THE
DAVIS CUP

THE DAVIS CUP

Edward C. Potter

South Brunswick and New York:
A. S. Barnes and Company
London: Thomas Yoseloff Ltd

Library of Congress Catalogue Card Number: 68-27208

A. S. Barnes and Co., Inc.
Cranbury, New Jersey 08512

Thomas Yoseloff Ltd
108 New Bond Street
London W1Y OQX, England

SBN 498-06665-7
Printed in the United States of America

Contents

THE
DAVIS CUP

I

Inspiration

Among all the sports trophies in existence today, the Davis Cup is the best known and the most sought after. Two unique characteristics are responsible for this. Tennis is a universal sport. It is played all over the world. Anywhere one goes, a tennis racket is a passport to friendly rivalry on the court, whether it be in a huge stadium or a jungle clearing. And the Davis Cup is distinguished from other trophies in that it is contested for by teams, rather than by individuals.

One must remember, too, that the game of lawn tennis is a youngster among sports. It is antedated by golf, skating, swimming, track and field, as well as such team sports as cricket, football and lacrosse. Though the game, as we know it today, is the descendant of an "invention" by a retired English Army officer, the rules, with only minor modifications, are those which governed the first lawn tennis tournament ever held.

Is it mere coincidence that the date of this tournament which began on July 9, 1877, and the birth date of the donor of the Cup, Dwight Filley Davis, who was born on July 5, 1879, are only two years apart? In May, 1881, the United States National Lawn Tennis Association was formed and the British Lawn Tennis Association followed in January, 1888.

Almost since the beginning there had been informal matches between players of the two countries. It remained for Davis to crystallize these rivalries into a world-wide competition which was not limited by the fact that the first two participants were England and America.

Davis came of a wealthy family from St. Louis, Missouri. He was educated in Eastern schools and learned the game at Magnolia, a Massachusetts summer resort. He and his doubles partner, Holcombe Ward, were members of the Harvard Class of 1900. They were runners-up in the National Doubles Championship of 1898 and held the title from 1899 to 1901. Ward was later to win the singles title in 1904.

In the spring of 1899, Davis with Ward and two other companions set out on a cross-country tennis tour. At that time, just after the Spanish

War, championship skill was concentrated on the Atlantic Coast, principally in the Eastern Universities. Yet California and other Pacific Coast states were not far behind. The Hardys and Whitneys were supreme in Northern California, while Lewis Freeman was the leader in the Los Angeles area. It was time for the Easterners and Westerners to inaugurate intersectional meetings.

A better quartet to bring East and West together could not have been found. In addition to Davis and Ward, the National Doubles Champions, there was Malcolm D. Whitman, the Singles Champion from 1898 to 1900, and Beals C. Wright, who was then Interscholastic Champion and who was to win the National title in 1905 and the Doubles, with Ward, from 1904 to 1906. Their mentor and guide on their 8,000 mile trip was George Wright, Beals' father and a former baseball great.

Like many events which have marked the turning points of history, the genesis of the Davis Cup was partly the result of a brilliant idea and partly fortuitous. As Davis himself stated some years later, the western trip of the four Harvard students "resulted in great benefit to the game throughout the whole United Sates and abroad."

So, after consultation with his fellow travelers and with officers of the United States National Lawn Tennis Association, Davis ordered Shreve, Crump and Low, silversmiths of Boston, to make up 217 troy ounces of sterling silver into the great thirteen-inch-high bowl officially entitled International Lawn Tennis Challenge Trophy, but known wherever tennis is played as the Davis Cup. The deed of gift, which was accepted by the Executive Committee of the USNLTA at a meeting on February 21,1900, made no restriction as to the number or geographical location of the competitors. From the very first the International Lawn Tennis Championship was thrown open to all the world.

This confidence in the future of tennis was justified almost from the start. It was as if some sage mechanic, looking over a creaking and unbalanced machine, discovered what was missing to make it run and added the one tiny cog which caused the contraption to function in a way undreamed of by its maker.

So far as America was concerned, past contests of an international nature had been between individuals. Sometimes the visitors had the official blessing of their Association but tests were confined to participation in singles or doubles events. No such thing as a contest of teams representing different nations had been imagined, though such a dream had long occupied the thoughts of Dr. James Dwight, one of the fathers of the game in the United States and President of the USNLTA for twenty-one years. Dwight was one of the young men who played at

Nahant on one of the first "sets" imported into the United States. He was the mentor and doubles partner of the first American Champion, Richard D. Sears, who held the title for seven years until his voluntary retirement.

It was not long after his first win of the Doubles Championship that Dwight's thoughts turned to England and the possible rivalry of his protege and the English champion, Willie Renshaw. So that there might be some semi-official imprimatur on their pretensions, Dwight organized a special doubles competition, the winner to be tagged America's representatives for the Championship of the World. Unfortunately, Dwight's plans miscarried when he and Sears were beaten by Joseph and Clarence Clark of Philadelphia. All he could do was to send the Clarks on their way with the Association's blessing.

The Clarks were welcomed with great deference when they arrived in England in the spring of 1883. The official tests were held at Wimbledon, the first two days after the close of the championship and the second a week later. In the first match the Clarks carried the Renshaws to 8-6 in the second set and won the third. In the second match they won only eight games.

Dwight was not disappointed. But there must be no more experimenting. Early in 1884 he took ship for the south of France. On the Riviera he played against the Renshaws several times. He was by no means disgraced but his efforts to prove, even in handicaps, that he was the equal of the English players were fruitless. As a last resort he sent a call for Sears. If the unbeatable American champion could not do better it must be true that the Americans had something to learn.

Sears joined Dwight at Cannes. They played on the Continent and in England until July, but their invasion was no more successful than that of the Clarks. When Livingston Beeckman, a lad of seventeen, reached the challenge round in 1886 and won the first set from Sears, Dwight began to realize that Sears could not go on forever. He wished to develop new blood which would succeed where he and Sears had failed and bring the Wimbledon Championship to America. Beeckman was ideal material.

Dwight took the youngster with him to the Riviera that winter and was bitterly disappointed in his protege's showing. Beeckman's interest in the gay life of the Cote d'Azur exceeded his desire to win on the courts. Dwight sent him home and went on to England alone. He was now on his way to forty and decided not to compete at Wimbledon. At home he and Sears won the Doubles Championship for the fifth time and Sears retained his Singles title. Shortly after this he hurt a muscle in his neck, had to have an operation and announced his retirement.

With Sears and Dwight no longer in the lists, a steady invasion of

English players commenced. The first was C. G. Eames, who played in several late-season tournaments with little success. He was followed the next summer by E. G. Meers, a veteran player and later indoor champion of England. Meers entered the American Championship and reached the semi-final. Here he was beaten by Oliver Campbell, a boy of eighteen. Campbell won the championship in 1890 and held it for three years. In 1892 Campbell went to England, played in five tournaments and was beaten by the sounder all-court game of his British rivals.

These frequent interchanges of visiting players cemented the friendly relations existing between the two groups. The English rather looked down on American tennis as a sort of poor relation to the Wimbledon brand. The visits of Eames and Meers were not regarded as conclusive. It remained to be seen what ranking English players could accomplish on American courts.

The first to try his luck was Manlove F. Goodbody, an Irish player of some note. He came first in 1893 but was out of practice and made no impression. He returned in 1894 and competed in the Championship. He beat all the American players and won the all-comers'. In the challenge round he was defeated by Robert D. Wrenn, the standing-out champion.

The visitors of 1895 were two Irish players, Dr. Joshua Pim and Harold S. Mahony. Pim was English Champion in 1893 and 1894 and Mahony was to succeed Wilfred Baddeley as Champion in 1896. In an invitation tournament at West Newton, Mass., Mahony beat all the American players while Pim lost only to Hobart. The return visit of William A. Larned to England in 1896 when he played close matches with Baddeley and Mahony and was ranked No. 6 in England marked the point where American and English players could be considered on a par.

This became even more evident in 1897. Dr. Dwight had corresponded early in the year with W. H. Collins, Secretary of the English LTA, suggesting a team match between American and English players. Negotiations dragged along to the point where it was too late to arrange such a match, so Dwight suggested that three English players be sent over to play in the American summer tournaments. While the LTA decided not to send an official team, three ranking players came over unofficially and took part in four American tournaments. They were Mahony, who had just lost his Championship to R. F. Doherty and was ranked No. 2, Dr. W. V. Eaves, ranked No. 3, and Harold A. Nisbet, No. 16. Eaves was at the top of his career. Nisbet had won the all-comers' Doubles with Doherty. They played in four tournaments but only gave a good account of themselves in the Championship. At Newport, Mahony was in poor form and lost in an early round. Eaves and Nisbet came through to the all-comers' final. Eaves confirmed his superiority over his compatriot. The challenge round against Wrenn went to five sets. Several times Eaves was close to winning, but Wrenn once more turned back a visiting challenge.

International contests were now almost an established institution. Clarence Hobart, American Doubles Champion in 1893 and 1894, went to England in 1898. He was beaten in the semi-final of the Singles by H. L. Doherty and won the all-comers' Doubles with Nisbet. He returned in 1899 and repeated his doubles win but lost to Roper Barrett in the singles. The English no longer looked down on American standards of play but wished to have a conclusive test. It only remained for Wrenn and Larned to go to England. This was indeed the plan, and an international match was arranged to follow the 1898 Wimbledon championships. But in April, 1898, the troubles in Cuba leading to the blowing up of the battleship *Maine* in Havana harbor culminated in the United States declaring war on Spain. Leonard Wood and Theodore Roosevelt organized the Rough Riders. American youth responded to the call of adventure. Leading tennis players volunteered for the regiment. Among them were Larned and Wrenn.

The troops returned from Cuba within the year, but the hardships of the campaign in the tropical, malaria-ridden marshes sapped the strength of many. Larned was gravely ill and did not fully recover until 1901. Wrenn's game had lost the sparkle and vim which had hitherto characterized it. When he came back to the championship in 1899, a new and younger Champion, Malcolm Whitman, was in the saddle. College boys like Whitman, Davis, Ward and Wright had taken leading places in the First Ten. The volleying game of which Wrenn was a master was falling back before Whitman's sounder all-court tactics. The classic game of the Dohertys was sweeping everything before it in England. It is doubtful, even if Wrenn had been able to regain his old form, if he would have been successful in an English invasion. Even at home he was a back number. His attempt at a comeback was futile. He won fame in doubles later on but he was never again ranked in the First Ten. A new era of international competition was about to dawn.

2

Challenge

Soon after the Davis Cup was accepted by the USNLTA, negotiations were opened with the English LTA with a view to holding the first match during the summer. England was engaged in the Boer War. Many first class players had enlisted. The English singles champion, Reginald F. Doherty, and his brother, Hugh Laurence Doherty, holder with his brother of the doubles title, could not make the trip to America. The team selected was composed of Arthur W. Gore, runner-up to Doherty in 1899; Herbert Roger Barrett, runner-up with Gore in the All-Comers' doubles the same year; and Ernest D. Black, champion of Scotland.

There was no doubt who would be the American team. Whitman and Davis were Nos. 1 and 2, and Ward, No. 7, was doubles champion with Davis. Whitman's close application and intensive study of tennis strokes and tactics convinced him that the reason the English champions had always beaten American vistors was their greater skill in the all-court game. The Americans, on the other hand, had been content to concentrate on the service and volley. Davis based his conception of the game on his speed and strength rather than on finesse. He had the most powerful straight service seen up to that time. He had sound ground strokes and a steady volleying game. His partner, Ward, was short and slight and the greatest exponent of the "American Twist" service. He was able to put such weird angles into the bound of the ball that it was practically unplayable. Whitman's twist service, with a reverse break, was fully as difficult to handle as Ward's. He had a long reach and was extremely difficult to pass, yet he did not advance to the net blindly. He prepared his opening by accurate backcourt strokes.

The Longwood Cricket Club, near Boston, was the scene of the first challenge round. The dates were set for Wednesday, Thursday and Friday, August 8, 9 and 10. The schedule, which has been followed to this day, provided for two singles matches the first day, a doubles match on the second, and two more singles on the third day with the players changing opponents. The Secretary of the English LTA informed President Dwight that the team would arrive at New York on the *Campania* on August 4 but that Barrett would have to sail for home on the 11th. The schedule was then advanced one day.

Due to a misunderstanding, no American official appeared to greet the visitors and, as no facilities for practice had been offered them, they decided to visit Niagara before proceeding to Boston. Their disappearance caused some anxiety to the Longwood officials, but when they finally turned up in Boston they were royally received and thoroughly beaten.

On the first day Davis beat Black 4-6, 6-2, 6-4, 6-4. Whitman made short work of Gore 6-1, 6-3, 6-2. Davis and Ward beat Black and Barrett in the doubles in three 6-4 sets. On the final day Davis and Gore played to a standstill, with Davis leading 9-7 9-9 when the match was called by rain. As the tie had been settled by the Americans' 3-0 lead and as Barrett had to return home, there was no further play.

"I often laugh to myself," Barrett commented, "that I journeyed some 6,800 miles to play thirty games." Yet his brief appearance on the courts did not deter him from criticizing almost every aspect of the American scene. "The ground was abominable . . .the net a disgrace to civilized lawn tennis . . .the balls were soft and motherly looking . . .the service quite non-plused us." At least, he admitted, "the spectators were most impartial and the female portion thereof not at all unpleasant to gaze upon."

British Isles challenged again in 1901 but defaulted when it was found that the Dohertys could not be included in the team. The LTA was determined that only their best players would be sent and in 1902 the Do's, accompanied by Dr. Joshua Pim and W. H. Collins, President of the LTA, came to America. Though Reggie ("Big Do") lost his singles title in 1901 when he was beaten in the challenge round by Gore, Laurie ("Little Do") regained the championship for the family in 1902. During the summer of 1901, Ward and Davis visited England and competed at Wimbledon. Their speed and their twist service created a sensation. They lost only one set on the way to the challenge round, where the Dohertys beat them in a hard match. It was the first time any overseas player or team had gone so far. Their success did much to correct the English impression that the American victory of 1900 had been a fluke, won under conditions that manifestly favored the home players.

The Dohertys were not only truly great singles players, having won the English title nine times between them with only one break. They were also one of the most perfect doubles teams of all time. Yet they were not supreme in any single department. Others have had stronger ground strokes or more severe services or more deadly volleys. But there have been few players who combined *all* these elements to the same degree of perfection as the Dohertys. There have certainly been more none who added to exemplary technique a character of personal charm and sportsmanship which has earned them fame as knights of the court.

Flushed with the success of its team in the 1900 contest, the USNLTA named Ward and Davis for the doubles without hesitation. Whitman had not defended his singles title in 1901 and William A. Larned, runner-up to Whitman in 1900, succeeded him and repeated against Beals Wright in 1901. Whitman was prevailed upon to join the team and to play one of the singles with Larned. The Crescent Athletic Club at Bay Ridge, Brooklyn, was chosen as the venue for the match.

For the first and only time in Davis Cup history no admission was charged. As a result the crowds ranged from 5,000 to 10,000. It was a long, tiresome ride in trolley cars over the Brooklyn Bridge from New York to Bay Ridge, although some of the spectators came by ferry across the Bay. The match was scheduled for Thursday, Friday and Saturday, August 6, 7 and 8, the week before the championships at Newport. After their arrival the English team went to Longwood for practice. Pim had long been absent from top fight competition. He had put on weight and, when the team left England, was considered as only a substitute. But he practiced hard, lost some twenty pounds and regained much of his old form. When the draw was made Whitman and Larned were named for the singles. Captain Collins decided to play Reggie Doherty and Pim in the singles and to hold out Laurie Doherty for the doubles. This caused Laurie to remark, "Must be a jolly fine team. You haven't asked either the Irish or English champion to play."

As in 1900, the opening singles were played simultaneously on adjoining courts. Larned led R. F. Doherty 6-3 6-2 and Whitman led Pim 6-1 6-1 when a thunderstorm interrupted play. The rain came down in torrents and play was over for the day. It was decided to finish the two matches the next morning rather than have the contest carry over the weeek-end. When the play was resumed, Pim got going and took the third set from 6-1. But it was only a brief resurgence, for Whitman came back to win the fourth at love.

A similar change occurred when Larned and Doherty took the court. R. F.'s play improved greatly, while Larned seemed to be bothered by the wind. Doherty won the third set 6-3, evened the match with a 6-4 win of the fourth, and took the fifth by the same score. Each side now had a rubber apiece.

Because of Thursday's rain, instead of separating the four singles by a doubles, the morning's opponents merely changed sides in the afternoon

The first United States Davis Cup Team 1900. *Left to right:* Malcolm D. Whitman, Dwight F. Davis (donor of the Cup), and Holcombe Ward.

When the United States and Great Britain engaged in the second battle for the Cup, this huge gallery assembled to watch at the Crescent Athletic Club in 1902.

and went at it again. Larned by now had overcome his morning let-down and made short work of Pim. The play was chiefly from the backcourt and was characterized by hard driving. Larned had no bad patches of any length and maintained the pace almost from start to finish. His win at 6-3, 6-2, 6-3 put the American team one rubber ahead.

The fate of the Cup now hung on the outcome of the Whitman-Doherty match. If Whitman won, the Cup would go to America. If he lost, all would depend on the result of the doubles. As the Dohertys had beaten Ward and Davis at Wimbledon, a repetition of the result would have sent the Cup on a journey to England.

Whitman was clearly the better player on the form of the day. He varied his service between a slow, straight delivery and the reverse twist which Doherty, until near the end, could not fathom. He kept his opponent constantly on the move, working the Englishman out of position for openings. After winning the first set 6-1, Whitman met with sterner opposition in the second when Doherty led at 5-4. But Whitman increased the pressure, ran out the last three games for a 7-5 win and took the third set 6-4. The Cup was now safe for another year.

In spite of the fact that the final match had no bearing on the outcome of the tie, both teams played their hardest. Davis' serving and smashing were almost unreturnable in the first set. The Americans got a 3-0 lead with a service break and held it for the set at 6-3. Again they had a 3-1 lead in the second set, but the tables were turned in the 6th game and service held until the 18th game, when Davis lost his service for the set at 10-8. Once again Davis lost his service to give the Englishmen a lead in the third set for a 6-3 win. In the fourth the Americans tired rapidly, lost Ward's service, evened the score at 4-all, then lost Davis' delivery in the 9th game to give the match to the Do's.

In the championships the following week at Newport, the Doherty's once more beat Ward and Davis 11-9, 12-10, 6-4 to become the first foreign winners of an American title. In the singles, too, they made a strong impression. They were drawn in the same half and both came through to the semi-final. Laurie wished to give Reggie a chance to avenge his defeat by Whitman and defaulted to his brother. Reggie beat Whitman in four sets in the final and then challenged Larned, the standing-out champion. Larned, too, had a score to settle and defeated his Davis Cup conqueror 4-6, 6-2, 6-4, 8-6.

If Captain Collins erred in playing an old champion instead of a new one in 1902, the Americans made an even worse tactical error in 1903. Whitman had definitely retired from competitive play. Davis had retired from both singles and doubles. Ward, who was to become doubles champion with Beals Wright in 1904, was still searching for a replacement for Davis. For the singles Larned, the champion, was a certainty, but in considering whom to name to succeed Whitman on the team, the committee passed over Wright, No. 3, and Ward, No. 4, and selected the 1897 champion, Bob Wrenn. Bob and his brother, George, by virtue of their ranking as the No. 1 doubles pair, completed the team.

This time the English left nothing to chance. The Dohertys were now familiar with American conditions and unafraid of the American service, particulary as its three greatest exponents would no longer oppose them. Collins again captained the team and, although Harold Mahony was sent along as a spare, Collins was instructed to use the Dohertys for both singles and doubles.

The third challenge round was again to be held at Longwood, where every precaution had been taken to insure perfect playing conditions which had so lamentably been lacking in 1900. The Englishmen arrived early in August and commenced to practice at Nahant. There Reggie Doherty injured his arm. When the pain persisted up to the Monday before the Cup match was to be held, Collins called in a physician who told Doherty that there would be a grave risk that he might be sidelined for several weeks if he played on Wednesday, but that there was a good chance that he would recover sufficiently to play on Thursday if he gave the arm enough rest.

Here was a poser for Captain Collins. Should he name Mahony and run the same risk he had with Pim? Or should he name the Dohertys and take a chance that they would make up in later matches the loss of the first? He had no intention of playing Reggie on the first day. That would have been suicidal. He spotted the Americans one match by defaulting Reggie to Larned and leaving Laurie to even matters with Wrenn. Wrenn was no match for "Little Do." He failed to win a game in the first set, and his total of points in the first four games was two. He did better in the next two sets, but Doherty was not really threatened and pulled them out 6-3, 6-4.

Rain had fallen intermittently during the match and increased on Wednesday and Thursday so that Reggie had time to be treated and was able to play in the doubles on Friday and the singles on Saturday. The Wrenns justified their selection for the doubles, though they won only the third set. The Dohertys' victory at 7-5, 9-7, 2-6, 6-3 justified Collins' strategy.

The two last matches on Saturday were again played on adjoining courts. One can well imagine the confusion as, in the midst of a tense rally on one court, the adjacent galllery burst into applause over a fine

The doubles contest at the Longwood Cricket Club, August 9, 1900, was the third match played for the Davis Cup.

The American and British teams of 1903. *Rear:* G. L. Wrenn (U.S.), Captain Collins (G.B.), H.S. Mahoney (G.B.), R.D. Wrenn (U.S.). *Front:* H.L. Doherty (G.B.), W.A. Larned (U.S.), R. F. Doherty (G.B.).

shot made a few feet away. As Collins said afterward, the players "not only had the anxiety of their own match on their shoulders but could not help following the state of affairs in the other."

On the other side of the umpire's chair, Laurie was having an equally difficult time with Larned. Again it was the Englishman who drew first blood and the American who fought back to even terms. Now both matches were in the fifth set. The score was three-all between Reggie and Wrenn and four-all between Larned and Laurie. Laurie was serving with the score 15-40 for Larned, with his own service to follow. Doherty asked the umpire if his service had been good. The official looked to where a linesman should have been. The chair was empty. Dr. Dwight was the Referee. He was appealed to for a ruling. He cancelled the point and called a let. Larned, on his way to victory, was halted in his stride. Doherty won the replayed point, the game, set, match and Cup. The others, who had stopped to listen to the discussion, resumed. Reggie finished off with a second win.

Endless argument followed this incident. American partisans claimed that Dwight should not have reversed the umpire's decision and that Larned was robbed of a victory whose stimulus might well have encouraged Wrenn in his fight with the ailing Reggie. What with the deplorable conditions under which the first contest was played, the tactical errors which marked the second, and now the mystery of the missing linesman, the atmosphere which surrounded the infancy of the Davis Cup competition was not of the healthiest. But there is no question, nor has there ever been, of the merit of the Dohertys' performance. If there had been, it must have been answered at Newport. The brothers defended their doubles title and Laurie beat Larned in the singles. The Cup and both championships were in British hands.

3

The Cup Goes "Down Under"

With the Cup now across the Channel, 1904 saw the first entry of Continental nations. Austria, Belgium and France were the challengers. United States was unable to finance the sending of a team as there were only a few hundred dollars in the USNLTA Treasury. Austria was obliged to default, so only one tie preceded the challenge round.

Max Decugis was the real father of French tennis. He went to school at Twickenham in England and, when he was fifteen, won a handicap doubles at Brighton with Harold Mahony as his partner. He won the junior championship of England the same year and the interscholastic title in Paris two years later. His style combined the best elements of the well-rounded English game with the dash and impetuousness of his race. He was short, quick and wiry and knew his limitations without lacking courage. In 1902 Decugis won the first of his thirteen French doubles titles and in 1903 the first of his eight singles championships. Decugis' partner was P. Ayme, French singles champion from 1897 to 1900 and doubles champion in three of these four years.

The match was played at Wimbledon from June 27 to 29. On the first day Decugis beat de Borman 6-4, 5-3 retired with an injured arm. Lemaire evened the score with a 6-1, 6-0, 6-1 win over Ayme. The doubles went to five sets with the Frenchmen coming from behind at 5-7, 6-4, 0-6, 6-4, 6-2. On the final day, the Belgians won both matches, Lemaire beating Decugis, 5-7, 8-6, 0-6, 6-4, 6-2 and de Borman beating Ayme, 6-1, 6-3, 2-6, 1-6, 6-3.

The Challenge Round was played July 2, 4 and 5 with the defending British team winning a 5-0 victory in which the Belgians took only one set. Reggie Doherty had practically retired from singles play though he was still doubles champion with Laurie, who had succeeded him as the singles title holder in 1902. Frank L. Riseley, Laurie Doherty's challenger in the 1903 and 1904 championships, was named as the second singles player. Lemaire defaulted to H. L. Doherty and de Borman's win of the first set from Riseley was the Belgians' only consolation.

In America it seemed as if Larned were through. Laurie Doherty's two wins had robbed him of some of his confidence. He was unable to reach the final at Newport. Ward beat Clothier and took the title in Doherty's absence.

The meager treasury of the Association again precluded an American Challenge in 1905. Fred Anderson, a former Canadian champion who had come to New York some years before and was ranked in the first ten in 1905 and 1906, came to the rescue. He declared that he could raise the money to send the team abroad. He was given permission to try by the Association and obtained the necessary funds by public subscription.

The team which was sent was thought to be invincible. There was the champion, Holcombe Ward, William A. Larned, the champion of 1901 and 1902, the doubles champions, Ward and Beals Wright, and the runnerup to Ward at Newport, Clothier. Paul Dashiell was named Captain and Manager with instructions to use Ward and Larned in singles and Ward and Wright in doubles.

Austria, Belgium and France challenged again in 1905 and, besides United States, there was a new challenger, Australasia. Though the team sent to England contained only one Australian, the inclusion of three New Zealanders gave the combination its compound title.

The New Zealander who was best known in England was Anthony F. Wilding who had been sent to Cambridge by his father, an English athlete in the 70's, as the opening wedge to a cricket Blue or else the Wimbledon title. At first Tony was not much interested in tennis. Like many another he thought it was a sissy's game. Cricket and football, which he played at school, were more to his taste. But after his arrival in England, while spending some months at a cramming school, he beat his master and fellow students at tennis. He was told he should go in for the game at Cambridge.

Though he won his freshman tournament, he still believed cricket was the more robust sport. When he became honorary secretary of the varsity tennis team he found the club faced with a large deficit. It was his job to work it off. He arranged a series of matches with the Dohertys, Allens and other Cambridge graduates. During the 1905 season his team lost only one match. He was captain of the varsity, the savior of its finances, and was definitely committed to tennis as a career. His improvement was marked by his appointment to the Davis Cup team along with his fellow New Zealanders and a dark horse, Brookes, whom he had never seen and a little misprized.

Wilding was not the only one in England who had heard little of

Brookes. He was not a man to make vainglorious trumpetings of his ability. He was entirely self-taught. He was gifted with a marvellous touch and a sense of rhythm and position play above the ordinary. He developed practically alone his theories of stroking and tactics. When Eaves visited Australia in 1901 Brookes was introduced to the American twist service. He soon mastered it. He won the Victorian championship for the first time in 1902.

When Wilding learned of Brookes' arrival in England he went down to Beckenham to see what a dark horse looked like. He found him without much seeking. Brookes had come through the preliminary rounds and was to play Gore that afternoon in the challenge round. Wilding greeted his teammate with a hearty slap on the back. The slight, brown, rather wizened face of Brookes recoiled instinctively.

"So you're playing Gore, eh, old chap?" Wilding began without further preamble. "D'you think you've a chance of beating him?"

Brookes looked up at the six feet three of perfectly trained athlete who addressed him. In curt tones he replied without a smile, "Beat him? I'll be thundering surprised if I don't."

Both the American and Australasian teams entered the Wimbledon Championships which preceded the Davis Cup matches. Ward lost to Sydney Smith in the first round and Larned fell to Smith in straight sets in the quarterfinal. Clothier was beaten by Wilding and Wright by Gore. Brookes went through, beating Hillyard, Riseley and Gore without losing a set. In the final he met Smith and won at 7-5 in the fifth set, the last stroke being a net-cord. In the challenge round Laurie Doherty beat the Australian wizard 8-6, 6-2, 6-4.

Belgium defaulted to United States and the two second round ties were played at Queens Club, United States vs. France and Australasia vs. Austria, the first on July 13-15 and the second on July 17-19. Both resulted in 5-0 victories. Ward and Clothier played the singles for America and Ward and Wright the doubles against France, represented by Decugis and Germot, the 1905 French Champion. Germot won the second set from Clothier and that was all. For Australasia, Brookes and Wilding played the singles with Brookes teaming with Dunlop in the Doubles. The Austrians, Kinzl and von Wessely, won two sets, both from Wilding.

In the final, the same Australasian team lost to United States by a 5-0 score. Larned, like Wilding, was a driver by choice. Wright was an even more persistent volleyer than Brookes. But both the Americans were more seasoned players. Because of their similar tactics and because they were both left-handers, the opening match between Brookes and Wright was awaited with great interest. The American needed only four sets but the match lasted over two hours before Wright won 12-10, 5-7, 12-10, 6-4. Larned was in his best form. After pulling out a long first set at 14-12, he ran away with the others 6-0, 6-3. Wilding did not win a set from either American and Ward and Wright beat Brookes and Dunlop in four.

The Challenge Round was played at Wimbledon on July 21, 22 and 24 and the defending British team won a surprise 5-0 victory. In spite of Wright's fine play against Australasia, Captain Dashiell had his orders from home to play Ward and Larned in the Challenge round. While Reggie Doherty had now definitely retired from singles play, the British had another ace up their sleeves in Sydney H. Smith. A "one-stroke" player, like Gore, "Smith of Stroud" was a hard man to beat. His forehand was considered invulnerable and the Americans were coached to concentrate on Smith's backhand which was by far the weaker wing. He met Larned in the second match, after Laurie Doherty had pulled out a win from Ward after losing the first two sets. Though Larned, too, was beaten he had the consolation of winning the only set Smith ever lost in Davis Cup play. The doubles between the Do's and Ward and Wright was a titanic battle. The American champions won the first set 12-10 and also won the fourth 6-4. But the Dohertys were just able to run out the fifth set 8-6 after Ward accidentally hit the net in making an easy smash. With the Cup successfully defended, the last two matches had no bearing on the ultimate result and the British won them both.

Four of the five challengers of 1905 entered the contest in 1906. Belgium was the absentee and, as Austria and France defaulted, only Australasia and United States were left. For the Americans, Larned and Clothier were not named to the team, and Ward and Wright were sent to do the job alone. They were accompanied by Kreigh Collins and Ray Little, numbers eight and nine in the 1905 ranking. The night before the team sailed for England, Wright dined with his father at the Crescent Club. When he awoke next morning he sent for a bottle of cold mineral water but the bell-hop who answered his ring forgot to bring an opener. Wright tried to open the bottle with a toothbrush but the neck broke in his hand. He was badly cut. He called for help and fainted. The wound became infected on the ship. Only expert medical aid in London saved his life. One of the fingers on his right hand was amputated. He could not possibly play in the Cup matches.

There was not time to send home for reinforcements. Little replaced Wright both in singles and doubles. Considering that he was essentially a doubles player he acquitted himself well.

Brookes had returned to Melbourne to study the lessons of his English visit. Wilding stayed in Europe and perfected his strokes against British and Continental players. L. O. S. Poidevin, an Australian living in England, was named as Wilding's partner. The match was played at Newport, Wales on June 7, 8 and 9. Wilding won both his matches but both Ward and Little beat Poidevin. The doubles went to the American pair in straight sets.

The British team which met the Americans at Wimbledon the following week was the same which had successfully defended the Cup in 1905. It was again a 5-0 win for Smith and Laurie Doherty in the singles and the Dohertys in the doubles. Little put up a strong fight against H. L. Doherty, carrying the match to a fifth set. The doubles was also close, the Dohertys beating Ward and Little 3-6, 11-9, 9-7, 6-1.

Wilding went back to New Zealand that fall and won the Australasian singles and doubles championships. The Association lost no time in naming Brookes and Wilding for the Davis Cup team. The Americans were in a quandary. Wright's hand had healed, though he lost his championship to Clothier. He was willing to make the trip but Larned, Ward, Clothier and Little all pleaded other engagements. Karl Behr, a recent Yale graduate and number 5 in the ranking offered himself as a sacrificial lamb. He had beaten Larned a number of times and was a confirmed net-rusher. It was felt he and Wright would make a good team.

The British also had problems. Laurie Doherty had decided to retire. He not only declined to defend his Wimbledon title but he also would be unavailable for the Davis Cup team. His brother also decided to step aside and Gore and Barrett of the original 1900 team were chosen to defend the Cup. At Wimbledon Wilding met Wright in the first round and won in four sets. His next opponent was Brookes. The match went to five sets. It was the only time Brookes had to go so far. He was even more devastating than in 1905. He beat Gore in straight sets to reach the challenge round and, in Laurie's absence, won the championship to become the first overseas player to do so.

Two weeks later, on the Wimbledon center court, the Australasian team met the Americans. Brookes got his revenge on Wright but Wright made up for this by beating Wilding, The Americans won the doubles in five sets and the tie hinged on the fifth match. The Americans in the stands cheered when Behr took the first set from Brookes. They sat silent again as Brookes swept through the next three.

In the Challenge Round, played on July 20, 22 and 23, the Australasian players won both the first day's singles. In the doubles a Wimbledon battle was refought. Brookes and Wilding started off as if they were going to repeat their previous victory. They won the first two sets and led 5-3, 40-15 on Brookes' service in the third. Barrett was a fighter who never quit. He pulled the match out of the fire. The crowd went wild on the last day when Gore evened the score by beating Wilding. But Brookes chilled the English ardor as he had stifled American exuberance. He smothered Barrett 6-2, 6-0, 6-3 in the deciding match. When he sailed for home he carried with him not only the Wimbledon triple crown–singles, doubles and mixed doubles–but also the Davis Cup, the emblem of team supremacy.

4

The Interim

The Cup was now in Australasia where it was to remain for the next five years. The distance to the Antipodes was so great and the expense of sending a team so far beyond the limited budgets of nations which saw no possibility of a triumph, that only the two previous holders – the United States and the British Isles – entered the lists.

Wilding spent another winter on the Riviera and another summer in England in 1908. At Wimbledon he reached the quarter-final where he lost in four sets to Barrett. Gore, who had played in his first championship in 1890 and had won the title in 1901, beat Barrett in five sets in the All-Comers' final and took the championship by default in Brookes' absence. Wilding then packed his kit for home to defend the Cup he had helped win and to take his examinations for the New Zealand bar.

As the Challenge Round was scheduled to be played at Melbourne late in November, the British Isles agreed to meet the American team at Longwood in September. As none of the old standbys was available, Major J. G. Ritchie and James Cecil Parke were chosen as the British team. Ritchie had been a prominent figure since 1898 and Parke was the Irish champion.

The United States had no difficulty in naming its team. Larned and Wright, the champion and runner-up, were to play the singles. Fred Alexander and Harold Hackett, doubles champions, were to team in the doubles match.

Once again the two opening singles were played simultaneously on adjoining courts – Larned vs. Parke and Wright vs. Ritchie. While Larned won his match 6-3, 6-3, 7-5, Ritchie surprised everyone by taking Wright into camp with the loss of only six games. Basing his strategy on playing to Wright's backhand and then getting to the net, Ritchie effectively stifled Wright's net-rushing by keeping him in the backcourt.

Hackett and Alexander won the doubles in four sets. On the final day, Larned beat Ritchie 4-6, 6-3, 6-2, 6-3 by greater steadiness. Wright, back in form, beat Parke after losing the first two sets and being down 5-3 in the third.

Though three friends accompanied them to Australia, the American team consisted of only Alexander and Wright without captain or manager. Apart from Larned, this was the strongest team the Americans could have selected and the Australasians set about their preparation in deadly earnest.

Two years before, Wilding had met a retired English army surgeon who was a fanatic on the subject of physical condition. Wilding became convinced that he and Brookes should follow a similar regimen. Brookes was amused at Wilding's earnestness but gave his consent. They rose every morning at seven for a cup of tea followed by a long walk. After breakfast they played three to five hard sets of singles. After lunch, more stroke practice and a few sets of doubles. Then rope skipping, baths, massage, dinner and bed. The treatment, however strenuous, proved beneficial. This was one of the most closely contested of all the Cup ties up to that time.

Brookes and Alexander played the first match, and when the Australian led 4-0 everything seemed to be normal. But Alexander then got into his stride and won the set at 7-5. It was the first set Brookes had lost in two years and he was to lose the fourth, too, before he was done with the pugnacious American. Wilding's match against Wright was a tale of lost opportunities. The New Zealander got away to a good start but the American's varied length began to have its effect. Wilding, notwithstanding his weeks of training, was soon leg-weary from running up for a short chop, only to see a lob sail over his head to the baseline.

The doubles was one of the game's great matches. The Australasians were almost within reach of a three set win. But Brookes lost his service in the twelfth game and the Americans won the set at 7-5. Their momentum also carried them to a win of the fourth at 6-1. Brookes had begun to fail physically and in the last game of the fourth set was broken through at love. Play had now lasted for an hour and ten minutes and the teams were tied at two sets each and nineteen games apiece.

Wilding was broken through in the second game of the fifth set and it looked like an American victory. But Brookes was now over his bad spell. Three times he saved points which would have given the Americans a commanding lead. Alexander again lost his service in the seventh game and Brookes brought the score to 5-3 on his service. Wright then won his service and Wilding reached 40-15, match point on his. He served a double-fault and Brookes was beaten by a lob. Alexander intercepted a winning stroke from Wilding after Wright fell and the score was deuce. Twice the Americans reached vantage but the Australasians deuced the score. Finally they reached match point and Brookes served it out for set and match.

That it was a vital point was made clear next day. Wright, playing one of the greatest games of his life, downed Brookes after a match in which the fifth set went to twenty-two games and after losing the first two sets to the Australian wizard. The teams were now two rubbers all. Alexander had sat in the dressing room listening to the shouts of the spectators and watching the ups and downs of Wright's match. He was a nervous wreck when he went on the court to play Wilding in the deciding encounter. He could put up only feeble resistance to Wilding's calm and well-controlled game.

Both the British Isles and the United States challenged again in 1909 and once more the British team came to America for the preliminary round. Parke was again a member of the British team and was accompanied by C. P. Dixon and William C. Crawley. Dixon was the better of the two newcomers. He had reached the All-Comers' final in 1901 and was in the last eight in 1908 and 1909. Larned and Clothier played the singles for the United States and Hackett and Little played the doubles. The match was played at Germantown on September 11, 13 and 14. Only the doubles was close, the Americans winning at 8-6 in the fifth set. All four singles were straight set wins for the Americans and the final score was 5-0.

An unprecedented situation now arose when it was learned that none of the leading American players, even those who had defeated the British, could go to Australia for the Challenge Round which was to be played at Sydney the last of November. To prevent a default, the USNLTA selected two California youths – Maurice McLoughlin and Melville Long – to make the trip.

McLoughlin was born in Carson City, Nevada, and learned the game on the public courts of San Francisco where he had been a ball boy when Davis and his friends toured the west in 1899. In the summer of 1909 he and Long toured the East and its famous grass court tournaments. Like Brookes on his first visit to England, McLoughlin was totally unknown. Like Brookes, he swept everything before him. He astounded players and public with his wicked forehand, his mad dashes netward, his deft volleying and his terrific smashing and serving. He reached the All-Comers' final at Newport where he lost to Clothier. He was nicknamed the California Comet and his style created a new school of play in America.

The two young players were in an extremely trying position when they faced Brookes and Wilding, who composed the Australasian team. They did not win one of the five matches and McLoughlin won the only set lost by Wilding. Yet personally they made a fine impression and were far from disgraced. As the famous writer "Austral" reported, "They treated us to an exhibition of hard, free hitting, of purely offensive play, such as we are wholly unaccustomed to; and they were so earnest, so spontaneously enthusiastic, so spry, agile and care-free, that they speedily established themselves as prime favorites and received the lion's share of applause from the spectators."

For the second time in its history there was a hiatus in 1910 in Davis Cup play. Both the United States and the British Isles were willing to challenge again if their tie could be played either in America or England. But the Australasian Association exercised its prerogative in insisting that the first round, as well as the Challenge Round, be held in New Zealand, and furthermore, recalling the 1909 experience, insisted on having a veto on the composition of the opposing teams.

South Africa joined the ranks of the challengers in 1911 but defaulted before playing a match. This left the British Isles and the United States to play for the right to make the long journey to New Zealand. The British wished to have the tie played in England, but a suitable date could not be arranged. So the West Side Tennis Club, which then had its grounds in Van Cortlandt Park at Broadway and 238th Street, held its first Davis Cup match. Dixon of the 1909 team was accompanied by Arthur Lowe and Alfred Beamish. Beamish, a strong doubles player, reached the Wimbledon last eight in 1910 and 1911, while Lowe reached the semi-final in both years. Larned, McLoughlin, Tom Bundy and Ray Little were the American team. Bundy was All-Comers winner in 1910 and McLoughlin in 1911, both losing in the Challenge Round to Larned, who was completing his seventh and last win of the American Championship. Little was doubles champion with Gustave Touchard.

This first tie held in New York City attracted galleries of 5,000 or more and the Americans had a comparatively easy 4-1 victory, the only British point coming when Dixon and Beamish beat Little and Bundy in the doubles.

Another strong American team – Larned, Wright and McLoughlin – set sail for New Zealand on November 1. The matches were to be held at Christchurch on December 29, 30 and January 1, but bad weather caused a postponement so that a tie which should have been played in 1911 actually did not commence until 1912. Wilding had won the Wimbledon title in 1910 and 1911 and was in no mood to take the long trip, even to his home town, when Brookes seemed capable of holding the Cup without him. So Heath and Dunlop were called on again and it was another 5-0 win for Australasia. Wright fell to Brookes in four sets and Heath inflicted the same score on Larned. When Brookes and Dunlop consolidated their victory with another four set win in the doubles, Larned, suffering from rheumatism and a sprained ankle, was replaced by McLoughlin and Wright defaulted to Heath. In spite of the fact that the Cup had already been lost, McLoughlin put up a stirring battle against Brookes, carrying the veteran to five sets and winning the plaudits of the gallery.

France challenged again in 1912 and was drawn against the British Isles in the first round, the United States having a bye. It was not until after Dixon and Barrett had beaten the French team of Gobert, Decugis and Laurentz that America decided not to send a team abroad. Wilding had won his third Wimbledon championship and again refused to go to Australia, so Brookes, Heath and Dunlop again formed the defending team. Dixon captained the British team which met Australasia at Melbourne at the end of November. His teammates were J. Cecil Parke, F. G. Lowe and Alfred Beamish.

When Brookes stepped on the court against Parke in the opening match, there was scarcely a person in the crowd who was not sure his man would win. Brookes won the first three games, then went to 4-1. Parke pulled up to 4-all with some magnificent passing shots and, after Brookes got a 6-5 lead, pulled out the set at 8-6. Even when Parke won the second set at 6-3, Brookes' ultimate success was still looked for. In the third set Parke took a 3-0 lead, went to 5-1 and stood within one game of the match. But Brookes pulled himself together as he had so many times before, and won six games running for the set at 7-5. But there was no flicker of dismay in Parke's attitude. He took Brookes' service in the first game and went right on to take the deciding set at 6-2. The final scores in this first match were 8-6, 6-3, 5-7, 6-2.

Dixon started hesitantly against Heath, losing the first set 7-5, then took the next three at 6-4 to give the British a commanding lead of two rubbers to none. The Australasians evened the score when Brookes and Dunlop beat Parke and Beamish in straight sets, 6-4, 6-1, 7-5, and Brookes beat Dixon on the final day 6-3, 6-4, 6-4.

After an interval of a quarter-hour, Parke and Heath came on the court for the match that would decide the fate of the Cup. Parke took the first two sets 6-2, 6-4. Heath improved in the third set, which he carried to 4-all, before Parke lifted his game and won the next two games for set, match and the Cup.

"Who won?" asked Parke at the end of the dinner on Saturday night. "I thought we did, but you all seem so delighted that I am bewildered."

5
Back to America Again

Now that the Cup was in England again, the challengers increased to a record seven. Besides the United States and Australasia, Belgium and France returned to the lists as well as South Africa, which had entered in 1911 but defaulted. Canada and Germany were the newcomers.

When the draw was made, Belgium received a bye into the second round. France vs. Germany, Canada vs. South Africa, and United States vs. Australasia were paired for the first round.

There was no chance that Norman Brookes would journey so far but Tony Wilding, the three-times Wimbledon champion, was available if the tie were played in England. However, when the USNLTA cabled the Australasian LTA offering terms for a match in New York, the offer was accepted whether or not Wilding would be a member of the team. When he preferred to remain in England, the Australasian team which was sent to America was headed by Captain Stanley Doust, with Horace Rice and A. B. Jones as his teammates. The tie was set for June 6, 7 and 9 on the courts of the West Side Tennis Club in Van Cortlandt Park, New York, where the 1911 contest had been held.

A few days before this tie commenced, Germany had beaten France by four rubbers to one at Wiesbaden. For the first time in its history, a Davis Cup tie was played on a surface other than grass. The inexperienced management also erred in several decisions which might have affected the results. The French relied on their singles players of 1912, Decugis and Gobert, and Germot replaced Laurentz as the third player. Otto Froitzheim, Germany's leading player, was incapacitated by an injured arm and the German team included Oscar Kreuzer, F. W. Rahe and Heinrich Kleinschroth. Gobert had beaten Rahe in the Wimbledon quarter-final in 1912 and had gone to the All Comers' final before losing to Gore. Decugis had also reached the semifinal where Gobert beat him, and the French pair had won the Wimbledon doubles in 1911 after beating Kleinschroth and Rahe in the third round. On the surface the odds favored the French, but Gobert was in the army and out of practice and only the permission of an obliging Colonel gave him a leave of absence.

Gobert opened against Kreuzer and his brilliant play won the first set 6-1. Kreuzer took advantage of Gobert's letdown and won the second set 6-4. In the third his lack of condition began to tell on Gobert and Kreuzer won the next two sets handily, 6-2, 6-3. It was at this point that the management committed its first error. The Decugis-Rahe match was not started until 6 P. M. It went to five sets and play was stopped at 8:20 P. M. with the score 5-all. Next day, when the match was resumed at 5 P. M., Decugis won the necessary two games to tie the score at one rubber all.

The doubles followed at 5:30 the same day and narrowly escaped going into a fifth set, which would have caused another postponement. But, in a thrilling match, Rahe and Kleinschroth beat Decugis and Germot 7-5, 6-4, 9-7. The first singles next day was started at 10:30 A. M. to avoid another late encounter, but the timing now was useless as Gobert was completely off his game and Rahe won easily in three 6-1 sets. With the tie already lost, Decugis defaulted to Kreuzer.

Another innovation marked the victory of the United States over Australasia by four rubbers to one when, for the first time, one singles match followed another instead of the two matches being played simultaneously on adjoining courts. McLoughlin and Williams were named for the singles, with Hackett teaming with McLoughlin for doubles. Doust chose Rice and himself for singles and paired with Jones in doubles.

Dick Williams was as much the antithesis of Maurie McLoughlin as Wilding was of Brookes. He was born in Geneva, Switzerland, and commenced to play in early childhood, first under his father's supervision, later at the hands of competent coaches. As early as 1910, when he was only eighteen, he won the Swiss Championship. His strokes were beautifully executed, particularly his backhand. He took the ball on the rise and so had the early advantage of the net position where his volleys were decisive. He crossed to America with his father in 1912 on the *Titanic*. Mr. Williams was lost but Dick was picked up by one of the lifeboats. He played the game more for satisfaction of realizing difficult strokes than for winning trophies. He tried for the lines unceasingly and on his good days was unbeatable. But his good days were not always the dates of his important matches.

McLoughlin and Rice came out for the first match on Friday. Rice was a small, left-handed man, dressed in knickerbockers. He was outranked by Jones in Australia and might not have been selected by Doust if Jones had been fit. McLoughlin's speed and aggressiveness were too much for Rice and the American won as he pleased 6-1, 6-3, 6-3. It was quite different in the Williams-Doust encounter. Williams was erratic and Doust steady and clever. Williams won the first two sets 6-4. Then Doust won the third with the loss of only one game. Williams was frequently in difficulty in the fourth set, but he finally won it at 7-5 to give United States a 2-0 lead.

Doust and Jones scored a fine victory in the doubles, beating McLoughlin and Hackett and coming from a two sets to one deficit to win in the fifth at 9-7. A heavy rainstorm interrupted play at the beginning of the second set, but the court was covered with a tarpaulin and play was resumed after an hour's delay.

On Monday, Doust made a fight against McLoughlin for two sets but it availed him little as McLoughlin won at 6-4, 6-4, 6-2. In the final match, Williams could do little that was right until Rice had put the first two sets away but, with the score 0-1 in the third, Dick found himself, ran off six games for the set and was never headed thereafter.

The third first round match, between Canada and South Africa, was played at Queens on June 19, 20 and 21. Two-man teams represented each nation – R. B. Powell and B. P. Schwengers for Canada and V. R. Gauntlett and R. F. LeSueur for South Africa. Canada won four rubbers to one, South Africa's only point coming from Gauntlett's win over Schwengers.

The American and Australasian teams sailed for England on June 12. Both were entered at Wimbledon as well as members of the other Davis Cup challengers. McLoughlin, still tottering on sea-legs, played Barrett in his first Wimbledon match. The Englishman drew out the struggle to an 8-6 fifth set, but once McLoughlin had crossed this hurdle he improved in every match he played. He beat Williams, Ingram, Parke and Doust (in the All Comers' final) without losing a set to any of them and reached the Challenge Round against Wilding the idol of the crowd.

Wilding, as usual, had trained hard. He had also noticed the improvement in McLoughlin's game since they met in Sydney in 1909. Always an admirer of the Dohertys, he recalled how Laurie had beaten Brookes. He followed the same plan against his challenger. McLoughlin knew no other style than to dash for the net after every service. He was often foot-faulted for his eagerness but came within a point of winning the first set. Wilding stood in to the most crushing deliveries and blocked them back for clean passes. Wilding was at the top of his game in the second set, but he had to call on every reserve of finesse and power in the third when McLoughlin came from behind and again needed only one point for the set. Once more Wilding stood in to the service and took the match in the eighteenth game.

The Americans had less potent opposition in the Davis Cup. Both semi-final matches were played on the same days – July 10, 11 and 12 – Canada vs. Belgium at Folkestone, and United States vs. Germany at Nottingham. The question of venue arose again when the Germans wished the tie to be played at Wiesbaden on hard courts. The Americans were unwilling and the British Isles, as Champion and manager, decided on Nottingham.

At Folkestone the Canadians fielded the same two-man team which had won from South Africa. Belgium relied on Paul de Borman, a member of its 1904 team, with A. G. Watson as the second singles player and W. H. du Vivier for the doubles with Watson. Powell beat de Borman in three easy sets, almost entirely from the baseline. Schwengers beat Watson equally easily and Canada also won the doubles without the loss of a set. On the final day de Borman won the first set from Schwengers and made a good try for the second. When Canada won for a 4-0 lead, Watson defaulted to Powell.

Froitzheim had by now recovered from his sore arm and was the mainstay of the German team. He was a tall, thin right-hander. He had developed the art of backcourt driving to such a degree that he could put the ball on a handkerchief anywhere in the court. His regularity was that of a pendulum. Kreuzer was a left-hander and second to Froitzheim in Germany. Rain was falling when Williams and Kreuzer took the court for the first singles. Williams wore spikes which gave him better footing than the German. He won the first set quickly at 6-4 and the second at 6-2. After leading 2-0 in the third, Williams had a bad lapse and Kreuzer won it 6-4. The fourth set was all Williams. He went out for the kill and Kreuzer won only one game.

The second match between McLoughlin and Froitzheim was quite different. In spite of his injured arm and his lack of practice, Froitzheim won the first two sets 7-5, 6-2. He handled McLoughlin's service very well, standing back and bringing off many passing shots. Froitzheim continued his mastery in the third set, reaching 2-0 before McLoughlin took things in hand. Noting that the German was tiring, McLoughlin speeded up his offensive, won the third set with a run of six games, and took the fourth and fifth quite easily.

The doubles match, a very fine one, was won by McLoughlin and Hackett from Rahe and Kleinschroth in four close sets. The Germans won the second set and carried the fourth to a 5-2 lead. Then Hackett, who had been playing poorly, stiffened his game and the Americans took set and match at 8-6.

On the final day Williams played a brilliant match against Froitzheim,

British and American Doubles teams of 1913. *Left to right:* Barrett and Dixon (G.B.), Hackett and McLoughlin (U.S.). Courtesy *World Tennis)*

winning the last three sets with the loss of only 5 games after losing the first at 7-5. With the score now 4-0 for the United States, Wallace Johnson substituted for McLoughlin and beat Kreuzer in four sets for a 5-0 win.

The final round between Canada and the United States was played at Wimbledon on July 18, 19. Williams beat Schwengers in straight sets. McLoughlin did the same to Powell. When Hackett and McLoughlin beat the Canadians 6-3, 6-3, 12-10, the last two singles matches were abandoned. The United States was once more in the Challenge Round.

The British Isles named their two aces – Parke and Dixon – for the singles, and Barrett and Dixon, the Wimbledon champions, for the doubles. The tie was played on the Wimbledon Centre Court on July 25, 26 and 28.

McLoughlin met Parke in the first singles and the Irishman reversed his Wimbledon defeat with a five set win over the "Comet." In the first set McLoughlin was within a point of a 5-3 lead with his service to follow, but Parke saved it although McLoughlin eventually won the set at 10-8. In the second set, McLoughlin lost his service at 5-all and Parke took the set 7-5. Parke won the third set 6-4. Then, after a bad start in the fourth, he let it go to the American 6-1. Parke began service in the fifth set. His passing shots kept McLoughlin off balance as he came in. He won the American's service in the fourth game and went to 4-1. McLoughlin recovered and got to 3-5. McLoughlin won Parke's service in the ninth game and evened the score by winning his own for 5-all. With McLoughlin serving in the twelfth game, the end came. A perfect pass for 15-40 and an out by McLoughlin ended the match.

When Williams came out to meet Dixon, both men realized the outcome of the tie depended on their match. Williams was 22, a hard and daring hitter. Dixon was 40, a master of craft. The natural style of both men, their greater variety of stroke, and the fact that the game was not dominated by the service made for a far more entertaining match than the first. Williams won 8-6, 3-6, 6-2, 1-6, 7-5.

The British got off to a good start in the doubles, winning the first set 7-5. Then after losing the second 6-1, they came back in the third to take it 6-2. But they were unable to withstand the terrific pace of McLoughlin's serves and smashes and the crafty generalship and steadiness of Hackett. Neither Barrett nor Dixon could smash the American's lobs with finality, while Hackett was content just to keep the ball in play and wait until a lob came to McLoughlin, who made no mistakes.

The luck of the draw brought Dixon against McLoughlin in the first singles of the final day. Dixon held his own to 6-all in the first set, but that was all. McLoughlin took this set 8-6 and the next two 6-3, 6-2.

Though the cup had now been won, Parke and Williams were still to play their match. The American won the second and fourth sets and played brilliantly. He was not consistent, however, and Parke, playing steadily and confidently, always had the match in hand and went out at 6-2 in the fifth set. Unlike Behr in 1907 and Alexander in 1908, Parke had wisely stayed away from the McLoughlin-Dixon match so that his equanimity was untroubled by the result.

6

On the Brink of War

When the 1914 entry list closed with the new Champion Nation, United States, six challenges had been received. Two were former Champions – British Isles and Australasia. The other four had been challengers in previous years – Belgium, France, Germany and Canada. Germany and France received byes. British Isles vs. Belgium and Australasia vs. Canada were drawn in the first round, but even before the British-Belgium match was played at Folkestone on July 7, 8 and 9, the American Committee received a cable from Germany: "Regret cannot send a team. Players not available." Dates and locations for the remaining matches were then set, leaving Germany out.

The results of Wimbledon, however, changed the Germans' mind. It was now time the disrupted Australian team were brought together. Brookes arrived on the Riviera early in April. Wilding was there, making mincemeat of his Continental opponents. Brookes met him twice and lost both times. He was rusty after the long sea voyage and went on to England. Wilding stopped off in Paris and won the World's Hard Court Championship.

Brookes was assailed by reporters on his arrival in England. They wanted to know why he had come. "I've been hearing down in Melbourne that Wilding is unbeatable," Brookes replied. "I've beaten him in Australia and thought I might here. So I came to see."

The last eight at Wimbledon consisted of Parke and Mavrogordato of the British Davis Cup team, together with Davson, Beamish and Gore; Germot of the French team. Froitzheim of Germany, and Brookes. Froitzheim beat Mavrogordato in one semi-final. Brookes beat Beamish in the other. In the final, Brookes won the first two sets and lost the next two. Before the fifth set commenced, Brookes revived his forces with a pint of champagne. They were at six-all and deuce when Froitzheim drove hard to Brookes' forehand. The return, apparently out, was scored as vantage for Brookes. Froitzheim was dispirited by this piece of bad luck and lost the set at 8-6 and the match. In the Challenge Round Brookes made good his boast. His strokes were little less potent than in 1907. Wilding seemed paralyzed before him. Brookes won in straight sets.

Froitzheim's close match with the Champion changed the Germans' plans. A cable was sent to President Wrenn indicating that a team would be sent if the nomination was acceptable. Brookes, as Captain of the Australasian team, replied in the affirmative but later, displeased by the arrangement of the schedule, wished to retract. It was then too late. The first round match between Australasia and Canada had already been scheduled for July 23, 24 and 25 at Chicago, with the winner to meet Germany the following week.

Meanwhile Parke and Mavrogordato, with Barrett in the doubles, had beaten the Belgians (De Borman, Watson and du Vivier) 5-0 without losing a set. In the second round, played at Wimbledon, the British beat the French team of Decugis and Germot 4-1. Mavro lost a set to Germot, Decugis led two sets to one against Parke, and the French beat Barrett and Mavro in four sets in the doubles.

Brookes and Wilding had no trouble with the Canadians, Powell and Schwengers, at Chicago, winning 5-0 with no set lost. In a sullen frame of mind they moved on to Pittsburgh, where the Allegheny Country Club had offered its turf courts and its splendid clubhouse and facilities for the tie, to be held on July 30, 31 and August 1. The tragedy at Sarajevo had occurred on June 28 and by the time the Australasian and German teams reached Pittsburgh, war was seen to be inevitable and the atmosphere was charged with emotion. To make matters worse, the Club had never held an event of this importance. Ballboys and linesmen were of doubtful competence. Brookes was annoyed that the Germans had changed their plans and upset his schedule. The final touch of unpleasantness was caused by the attitude of the crowd. It was completely and openly pro-German. Wilding and Brookes complained of the ballboys, the applause and other disturbing influences. Their petulance gave the spectators many opportunities to give vent to their partisanship.

It was known that the outbreak of war was only a question of hours. The Germans had announced that they would at once throw down their rackets and cease play. It was hoped by the Club and the spectators that the news would not be received until the last two matches were completed. The referee had many an anxious moment.

Brookes and Froitzheim played the first match. The German had every stroke working to perfection and got away to a 5-2 lead in the first set. The applause was overwhelming. Brookes' nerves were at the breaking point but he began to creep up little by little. Mad handclapping greeted every winning German stroke, a dead silence each marvellous volley of the

Australian. Serene, supercilious, the pendulum ticked on. But Brookes was still his master. After winning the first set at 10-8, it was all Brookes. Froitzheim had nothing left. Wilding beat Kreutzer with the loss of only eight games. The Australasians won the doubles 6-1, 6-1, 6-2. The Germans had been defeated.

But the third day's matches were still to be played. The president of the club feared a last-minute interruption and had all telephone communication cut off. The grounds were barred to newspaper men. During the afternoon, while Wilding beat Froitzheim and Kreutzer took a set from Brookes, news reached the Club that war had been declared. As the last ball was played, a megaphone announced the event to the silent crowd. The Germans hurried off to take ship for home. While the challenge tie was being played, their boat was stopped by a British warship. They were taken off and interned at Gibraltar. Later they were taken to England, where they were imprisoned until peace was declared in 1918.

There was now no time to lose and the Australasians hurried off to Boston for the final round at Longwood. Parke played one singles, A. H. Lowe replaced Mavrogordato as the second singles, and Parke took Barrett's place in the doubles with Mavro.

Brookes met Parke, and a repetition of their memorable meeting at Melbourne in 1912 was anticipated. Although the contest went to five sets, neither man was playing his best. With a 5-3 lead in the fifth set it appeared that Parke might have the victory in hand. Now Brookes knew that the time had come to stake all on aggression. He dashed for the net on every occasion and pulled out the set at 7-5.

Previously, Wilding had toyed with Lowe to win the first set 6-3 and gain a 2-0 lead in the second. Lowe won a game, then Wilding ran five in a row to take the second set and a 1-0 lead in the third. Wilding was suffering from the sultry heat and Lowe could have had the set for the asking. But he did not seem to understand how to volley. Wilding just kept putting the ball back and the games dragged on to 14-all, with the service being constantly lost at love. Here Wilding, almost on the point of collapse, made a final stand and took the last two games for set and match. After Brookes and Wilding won the doubles next day, the last two matches were cancelled and the Australians moved on to Forest Hills for the Challenge Round against the American holders.

The West Side Tennis Club had moved from its Van Cortland Park location and had built a Club House and turf courts at Forest Hills. Temporary stands seating 11,130 people were erected, and with those in and around the clubhouse and enclosure, the number of spectators was in excess of 12,000.

Wilding and Williams came out for the first match. Williams started off confidently and soon had a lead of 4-1. He again led at 5-3 but Wilding, playing carefully, waited for Williams' errors and took the set at 7-5. There was no improvement in Williams' game in the next two sets, which Wilding won 6-2, 6-3 for the first Australasian point.

It was nearly four o'clock when McLoughlin and Brookes came out for their long looked-for meeting. No one who saw that historic match will ever forget it, especially the tremendous first set which went to 32 games. It was a battle of youth and power against court-craft and experience. Only superb vitality and sustained skill enabled McLoughlin to come out ahead. The set lasted for well over an hour, and as it progressed the gallery sat spellbound. It did not seem possible that two men could make such shots and deliver such service as they did for a time long enough for three ordinary sets. The suspense as to which would crack first became so intense that at the end many of the spectators were limp.

To 9-all games went with service. The Australian had his chance in the eighteenth game when he reached 40-love on McLoughlin's service. But five times McLoughlin served his fast ball and never gave Brookes a chance to get his racket on the first three. The battle of services went on. The crisis came in the thirty-first game. Brookes, serving, reached 40-15 and then got advantage after deuce had been called. After several more deuces, McLoughlin finally got vantage and drove Brookes' service hard to his feet for the game. The next game was bitterly fought and reached deuce. Then McLoughlin served two aces and the set was his.

That set practically ended the match. Brookes had put his all into it, and although he fought on, it was only because he was a fighter and not because he had any expectation of winning. He lost his service in the third game of the second set and McLoughlin won it 6-3. At 3-all in the third set, McLoughlin made a last great effort and won the next three games for set and match.

The American selection committee had difficulty deciding who would be named to the doubles. McLoughlin and Bundy were the National Champions, but the Committee sought a stronger partner for McLoughlin. But Mac held out for his friend till the end and Bundy was named on the morning of the match.

While the loss of Bundy's service in the fourth game gave the first set to the challengers, he recovered in the second set, held up his end well and did some fine lobbing. McLoughlin, on the other hand, was worrying about Bundy, lost his service twice in the second set and played badly. After holding leads of 4-3 and 5-4, the Americans faded quickly and lost

R. Norris Williams, American champion in 1914 and 1916. (Courtesy *World Tennis)*

Maurie McLoughlin (right), the great American champion, winner over Brookes of Australia in an historic match. Parke of Great Britain is at left. *(Courtesy World Tennis)*

the set at 8-6. McLoughlin lost his service to open the third set, and if Bundy has not been as good as either of the Australasians, the match would have been over sooner. McLoughlin eventually found his touch toward the end, but it came too late. With Brookes dominating the play at the net, the challengers won the set 9-7.

Brookes and Williams met in the first match on the third day and Brookes quickly got a lead of 3-0. Williams served out the fourth game but was outclassed in the next three as Brookes won the set 6-1. In the second set it was not until the fifth game that Williams scored. He was making many errors and double-faults. Williams showed his real form in the seventh game, winning it at love, but Brookes ran out the set at 6-2.

A charge came in the third set. Williams won the first game and was now holding his own. At 7-all Brookes won Williams' service and it looked as though it were all over. But Williams staged a successful attack and won the set 10-8. The gallery went wild and was in commotion from the time Williams launched his attack. Williams ran to the dressing room as soon as set point was scored, but Brookes remained. The applause continued and intensified and Brookes was annoyed by it. He put his hands to his ears, which had the effect of redoubling the pandemonium. It was not until he took his hands away and went to the dressing room that the gallery calmed down. When play was resumed Williams had lost his touch. Brookes was grim and relentless and forced the fight, taking Williams' service in the ninth game for the set and match, which gave the Cup to Australasia.

With nothing now at stake, the match between McLoughlin and Wilding was an exhibition of almost perfect tennis between two contrasting styles. McLoughlin was full of fire and daring, always aggressive. Wilding varied his play to cope with the shots that came over to him and employed both speed and finesse. After winning the first two sets 6-2, 6-3, McLoughlin tired and Wilding took advantage of the let-down to win five games in a row. McLoughlin then won the next two games, but Wilding stood in to Mac's service and hammered it unmercifully, winning the third set 6-2.

This set-back and a change at the interval aroused McLoughlin to his former devastating form. After losing the first game he won the next four giving Wilding only two points in the four games. At 5-1 he lost a game at love, but in the eighth he pulled himself together for a final effort and took the set and match 6-2.

This was a fitting climax to the careers of both men. Soon after his return to England, Wilding joined up and, in the spring of 1915, lost his life at Neuve Chapelle. Even before Wilding fell, McLoughlin had reached the end of his road. The strain imposed on his frail physique by the great fight with Brookes was too much for him. His admirers sat stunned and unbelieving at Newport as he lost his American title to Williams. He made an abortive come-back in 1915 but he never reached the heights again.

7

New Faces: Tilden and Johnston

With the signing of the Armistice in November, 1918, World War I came to an end. Since 1914, when Australasia had again become the Champion Nation, there had been no Davis Cup play. The Cup remained in New York as German raiders were wreaking havoc on Allied shipping and it was felt that the trophy would be safer in America.

While the Allied statesmen were drafting the treaty of Versailles, the shattered remnants of their armies were entraining for the demobilization camps. Those who exchanged racket for rifle in 1914 were sobered by the reflection that many of their comrades would face them no more on the courts. Wilding was gone, and Powell and others of lesser rank. Some, like Decugis, had reached maturity before the war. They were old men now. Others, like Gobert, had wasted four years of their prime. Only the Americans had come through practically unscathed.

For the players of the Central Powers, even the Armistice did not spell peace. They were victims of the hatreds engendered by the war. They were banned from the sanctioned tournaments of the International Federation and from participation in Davis Cup play. For several years German, Austrian and Hungarian players could compete only among themselves. The new nations, created by the treaty – Czechoslovakia, Poland and Yugoslavia – were admitted to the governing body of the game.

It was not until 1917 that the United States made a belated entry into the war. Until then, National and other tournaments continued without interruption. McLoughlin, in spite of his loss to Williams in the Championship, retained his Number One ranking, with Williams at Number Two. At Number Six was a young Californian, William M. Johnston, who had made his first appearance in the East the previous year. While McLoughlin and Williams were in England, Johnston won the Longwood Bowl and surprised the spectators with the sound character of his strokes.

Johnston was a small, featherweight lad who wore a white cap pulled down over his red hair. His Western forehand was hit with a full sweep of the racket and a great curving follow-through. The ball went hurtling down the line or crosscourt in the most perfectly orthodox form. Not only that, but his backhand belied the tradition that left-side strokes were unknown in California. There was nothing lethal about his service, although it was hard, well-sliced and accurately placed. His volleying was deadly but he came to the net only after careful preparation. Johnston's strokes were still in embryo but even a tyro could see that there was little of McLoughlin about him. He was a perfect exponent of the classic style of the Dohertys.

By the summer of 1915 Johnston had brought his strokes closer to perfection. By the time the Championships came along, he had adjusted his game to the strange surface. In the semi-final he avenged his 1914 defeat by Williams and met McLoughlin in the final. Mac won the first set at love, but it was a last display of his might. Johnston tamed the whirlwind with the beautiful symmetry of his strokes.

In 1916 Johnston was the standard-bearer of the California succession. But in the Championships he again met Williams in the final. For four sets there was little to choose between them. In the fifth the Californian took a 3-0 lead. Once more Williams' inspired touch came back to him and he pulled out the match.

When the United States entered the war in April, 1917, the Championships were abandoned and a "Patriotic tournament" was held instead. Johston joined the Navy. Williams got a commission in the Army. The Patriotic tournament was won by R. Lindley Murray, another Californian whose abilities as a chemist exempted him from military service.

The Championships were resumed in 1918 and Murray again won the title. His opponent in the final was a lanky Philadelphian of 25 named William Tatem Tilden II who had never had a First Ten ranking and who was generally considered to be "one of those promising players who never arrive."

Tilden was nineteen when Williams beat him in straight sets in the 1912 Pennsylvania Championships. At that time his strokes were rudimentary. He had the beginnings of a cannonball service and a forehand of tremendous pace. Williams' accuracy played havoc with Tilden's speed. He learned that control was more important than a berserk fury of attack. He set about practicing control and kept away from tournaments outside his home district.

In 1913 he partnered Mary Browne to win the mixed doubles championship. This performance earned him a place in the 31 to 40 group in the national ranking. He was unranked in 1914 and dropped to the 61

William M. (Little Bill) Johnston. (Courtesy *World Tennis)*

William T. Tilden, 2nd seven times U. S. champion. (Courtesy *World Tennis)*

to 70 group a year later. By 1916 he was satisfied that he might make some impression on the leaders. He was quickly disillusioned. Murray beat him at Seabright and in the Championships he went out to Harold Throckmorton in the first round. In the 1917 Patriotic Tournament Murray beat him again.

Tilden was exceptionally tall and had a tremendous reach, but he was not robust. He had outgrown his strength and was unfit for active war service. He enlisted in the Medical Corps and when the regular Championships were resumed in 1918, he won the Clay Court title. In the Championships at Forest Hills he again met Murray in the final and the Californian's greater experience earned him another victory. Tilden had now climbed to No. 2 in the national rankings.

Johnston had now returned from the war and in 1919 Tilden met him three times. Johnston won in the Clay Court Championships and lost in the East-West matches and at Newport. They met again in the final at Forest Hills. They were the outstanding players of the year and a hair-raising struggle was predicted. In view of his Newport win, Tilden was a slight favorite. But Johnston exploited Tilden's weak backhand with his terrific forehand drives and won back his title in straight sets. There were few among the onlookers who did not remark, "It took Little Bill to show up that big stiff."

Within a very few months after the signing of the Armistice it was decided to resume the Davis Cup contests, and the first post-war Championships were held at Wimbledon. As the United States had suffered the least of any of the Allied nations from the war, it was decided not to challenge for the Cup in 1919. The only ranking American who played at Wimbledon was Charles S. Garland, who was ranked No. 8 in 1918. The Australasian Champions were well represented by Pat O'Hara Wood, R. V. Thomas and Gerald Patterson, not to mention the standing-out title holder, Norman Brookes. Patterson, on his first visit to Wimbledon, became the first post-war Champion, beating Gobert, Ritchie, Kingscote and Brookes without the loss of a set. On their way back to Australia, Brookes and Patterson won the American doubles title and played in the singles, where Johnston beat Patterson while Tilden beat Brookes.

For the Davis Cup, Australia received challenges from Belgium, British Isles and France, plus a belated one from South Africa which necessitated reopening the draw.

France and Belgium played the first tie at Brussels on July 16 and 17. Decugis and Laurentz represented France and de Borman and Lammens played for Belgium. The result was an easy 3-0 win for the French, the last two singles not being played.

The British Isles met South Africa at Eastbourne on August 25, 26 and 28. South Africa fielded a team of soldiers, all new to international competition. They were Louis B. Raymond, George H. Dodd, H. I. P. Aitkin and Brian I. C. Norton. Only the first three actually played, Norton being held in reserve. The British relied on their pre-war men, Mavrogordato, Kingscote and Roper Barrett, and they had little difficulty taking a 4-1 victory. In the opening match Mavro beat Raymond in five sets after being down two sets to one. The South African stubbornly contested the fourth set, which he lost at 8-6. Mavro then took the final set 6-1.

Kingscote had an easier time with Dodd in the second rubber, winning about as he pleased, 6-3, 6-3, 6-2. When Barrett and Kingscote beat Dodd and Aitkin in the doubles, the tie had been won but the remaining two matches were played on Monday. Mavrogordato lost to Dodd in five sets after two hours' play for South Africa's only tally. Kingscote then beat Raymond after the South African had won the first set at love by aggressive play.

The final round, Britain vs. France, was played at Deauville on a hard court on September 25, 26 and 27. Barrett was Captain of the British team and he selected Kingscote and Percival M. Davson to play the singles with himself and O. G. Noel Turnbull for the doubles. For the French, Laurentz was substituted for Decugis, who had injured his back. Laurentz had not trained for a Davis Cup match and was the weaker member of his side. Gobert was the other French player.

On the first day, Gobert beat Davson in four sets and Laurentz, playing brilliantly, carried Kingscote to five, winning the first and fourth sets. Gobert and Laurentz renewed their pre-war partnership and overwhelmed the ill-assorted British pair, losing only one game in the first two sets. In the third set Laurentz tired and the Englishmen had a chance. They led at 6-5, but Laurentz recovered and the Frenchmen got home at 12-10.

A win of one of the two remaining singles would have put the French team in the Challenge Round, but it was not to be. Davson and Laurentz split the first two sets, then Laurentz won the third at 12-10 and the match seemed safely in his hands. But he tired in the fourth, which he lost 6-4, and he was then done. The final set went to Davson at love.

All now depended on Kingscote and he attacked from the start. Gobert played well, but his responsibilities affected him and Kingscote ran out the deciding rubber 6-4, 6-4, 7-5.

Officially the concluding tie of the 1919 contest, the Challenge Round was not played until January, 1920, at the Double Bay Grounds in Sydney. Kingscote, Arthur Lowe and A. E. Beamish composed the British team. Norman Brookes selected as his teammates Gerald Patterson and J. O. Anderson. Patterson, the new Wimbledon champion, was a Victorian – like Brookes. He had modeled his game on that of McLoughlin, and the battle-axe character of his attack created a furore as he breezed through Wimbledon. Brookes had planned to take the second singles himself, but in an Interstate match between Victoria and New South Wales he was beaten by Anderson. Anderson was over six feet tall and his style was awkward. His backhand was negligible but he had a mighty drive on the right wing.

In his first international match Anderson met Kingscote and lost in 55 minutes, 7-5, 6-2, 6-4. Lowe struggled gamely against Patterson and managed to take the third set, but the power of the Wimbledon title holder was too much for him. Brookes and Patterson teamed for the doubles and won from Kingscote and Beamish 6-0, 6-0, 6-2. Brookes was magnificent and his play was almost errorless. The Englishmen never could get started, try as they would. With the score 2-1, Patterson made the winning point when he beat Kingscote 6-4, 6-4, 8-6. Anderson finished brilliantly with a close five-setter over Lowe, 6-4, 5-7, 6-3, 4-6, 12-10. The Davis Cup was still in Australian hands.

8

The Two Bills

Tilden's defeat by Johnston in the 1919 American Championship was all the big fellow needed to convince him that his game was not all he imagined. He was always sensitive to criticism. His defeat and the comments which had reached his ears stung him. He'd been shown up, had he? Wait until next year. He'd do some showing up himself.

All winter he worked on his backhand. First he aimed for control. Then he put spin on it. At last it was as ready as his forehand to prove his theory that speed, or momentum, is not so important as pace, or speed off the ground. When he got his backhand near perfection he studied variety. Chops, half-volleys, short lobs, several new varieties of service were added to his repertoire. Another theory was about to be proved, the old one about giving your opponent the shots he doesn't like. By the time the active season commenced Tilden was, for the first time, a complete lawn tennis player.

Six challengers entered the contest for the Davis Cup in 1920. There was no longer reason for the United States to hold back. France, Canada, British Isles, Holland and South Africa were the other entries. British Isles and Canada drew byes. Holland vs. South Africa and United States vs. France met in the first round.

The Dutch played the South Africans at Arnheim June 11, 12 and 13. Norton was ill and could not play, and South Africa relied on Louis Raymond of its 1919 team and Charles L. Winslow. The Dutch, in the contest for the first time, also named a two-man team, C. J. Van Lennep and A. Diemer Kool. Holland's win was a surprise, but the determination of their men pulled them through for a 3-2 victory, Winslow, the best man in the singles, beat both Van Lennep and Kool in straight sets, but Raymond lost both his matches although he carried Van Lennep to five sets on the third day. The deciding match was the doubles, which the Dutch players won 6-2, 7-5, 6-4.

Knowing that it would be to the advantage of the European nations to play the preliminary rounds there, the USLTA expressed its willingness to send its team to Europe. Arrangements were made to have the team sail on May 29, but a strike in England delayed the ship and an Army Transport, through the good offices of the Secretary of War, got under way on May 27. The match against France had been set for Eastbourne July 8, 9 and 10, after Wimbledon, so the team had two objectives – Wimbledon and the Davis Cup.

Samuel Hardy, a Californian who had played against Davis and his companions on their visit to the Pacific Coast, was the Captain and was given a free hand in naming his players. Hardy had played on the Riviera and in England and was an ideal choice for the post. Yet Johnston and Williams were looked upon as the likely singles candidates, with Chuck Garland as Williams' doubles partner. As the No. 2 ranking player, Tilden was bidden to go along too, but merely as a possible replacement.

Tilden was glad to go but was dissatisfied with his role. He wanted to be star of the troupe. He had perfected his stroke but lacked the stimulus of match play. Shortly after the team arrived in England they moved on to Wimbledon.

Gerald Patterson was the defending champion. Parke and Kingscote, of the British Isles 1919 challenging team, were the Americans' strongest opponents. Yet neither Johnston, Kingscote nor Parke reached the round of eight. Johnston met Parke in the second round and was beaten in four sets. Tilden watched the match. He saw Johnston follow his usual plan of hitting weighty forehands to the corners to make his opponent run. A running drive was Parke's forte. When Tilden met the Irishman in the next round he was shrewd enough to try a different plan. He fed Parke the strokes he did not like, cramped his mobility and won easily.

In the fourth round he met Kingscote, who proved to be a tougher morsel. His better-rounded game often had Tilden in difficulty. But the American was improving with every match. He countered Kingscote's moves at vital moments and won in the fifth set.

The quarter-finalists turned out to be Mavrogordato, Williams, Shimizu of Japan, Willford, Tilden, Lycett, Garland and Blackbeard of South Africa. Williams was beaten in four sets but Garland won his in four. Shimizu made mincemeat of Willford, allowing him only three games. Tilden had another hard fight with Lycett but won at 7-5 in the fourth.

In the semi-finals, Tilden beat Garland in straight sets while Shimizu took four to dispose of Mavrogodato. Shimizu had perfected his game in India. His style was far from classic. His ground strokes were awkward but effective and his volleying was good. But he was no match for Tilden. He won only four games in each of the first two sets. Then Tilden twisted his knee. Shimizu carried the third set to twenty-four games before the limping American won it.

This accident put Captain Hardy on the spot. He did not wish to risk his best bet in the Cup by chancing further injury in the Wimbledon challenge round. On the other hand, Americans had been knocking at the All-England's door for close to forty years without ever getting in. Tilden had the knee massaged and taped and convinced Hardy that he was fit to play. He exploited Patterson's vulnerable backhand as Johnston had exploited his at Forest Hills. He stood in to the cannonballs and won in the fourth set. The American triumph was complete when Williams and Garland beat Johnston and Tilden in the doubles.

The weather at Eastbourne for the match with France was most unsuitable. Rain on the opening day, Thursday, permitted play for only a quarter of an hour and Monday's matches were called off for the same reason. Gobert and Laurentz were named to the French team, with Decugis and Jacques Brugnon in reserve. Tilden and Johnston played all three matches for the United States.

Johnston had a good lead against Gobert on Thursday and on Friday, when the court had dried, finished off the match at 6-3, 8-6, 6-3. Laurentz attacked Tilden from the start. He followed his service to the net and got his racket on nearly everything. The first set was his at 6-4. Tilden changed his tactics and fed Laurentz with slow, heavily cut shots kept low. He served well and mixed his game with such good judgment that he got the upper hand and won the next three sets, 6-2, 6-1, 6-3.

In the doubles on Saturday, Gobert and Laurentz were the favorites but Tilden and Johnston ran right through them, 6-2, 6-3, 6-2. Johnston was at his very best and Laurentz was the better of the Frenchmen. Tilden had little to do but toward the end he exploited his forehand destructively. The rain on Monday swamped the court and the last two singles were abandoned.

In the second round Holland defeated Canada by default and the United States met the British Isles at Wimbledon July 16, 17 and 19. Both sides fielded two-man teams, Parke and Kingscote for Britain and Tilden and Johnston for the United States. The result was a 5-0 win for the United States, although all the matches were hard-fought. On the first day Johnston beat Parke 6-4, 6-4, 2-6, 3-6, 6-2 and Tilden beat Kingscote 4-6, 6-1, 6-3, 6-1. The Americans were down two sets to one in the doubles but pulled it out 8-6, 4-6, 4-6, 6-3, 6-2. On the third day Johnston beat Kingscote 6-4, 4-6, 3-6, 6-4, 7-5, while Tilden took Parke's measure 6-2, 6-3, 7-5. Holland defaulted in the final round and the Australian goal was in sight.

W. T. Tilden, 2nd and Zenzu Shimizu. (Courtesy *World Tennis*)

As the first American winner of the All-England Championships, Tilden was a hero when the team came home. But the officials who had not seen him play belittled his achievement. The American Championships settled the question. Tilden and Johnston met again in the final. It was a different Tilden from 1919. He came through the preliminary rounds in less devastating fashion than Johnston, who was modest and self-effacing. He seemed weak and small beside the great height and pugnacious jaw of his opponent. He was the defending champion but he had the crowd's sympathy as if he were the under-dog. Many, of course, suspected Tilden's supremacy. Even Johnston wondered if he were to meet his master. The crash of a photographer's plane behind the stands at a crucial moment in the third set upset Johnston's concentration, but he fought doggedly on into the fifth set. Then, on match point, Tilden unleashed an unreturnable ace. Johnston ran gallantly to the net to shake his conqueror's hand.

The team to make the long journey to New Zealand was then got together. The Challenge Round was to be played on a specially prepared court on the Domain Cricket ground at Auckland, New Zealand. Set for late in the year, a two-day postponement due to rain caused the tie to run over into the New Year as the play took place on December 30, 31, and January 1.

There was some difficulty in settling on the American team. Tilden was a certainty, but for a long time it seemed as though Johnston would not be able to go. When these difficulties were removed it was found that Williams was obliged to change his plans. Captain Hardy invited Watson Washburn to accompany the team and he accepted. The four men sailed from Vancouver on the S. S. *Niagara* on November 15 and arrived at Auckland on December 3.

Brookes captained the Australasian team and chose Patterson, Heath and Pat O'Hara Wood as his teammates. But it was again a two against two encounter – Brookes and Patterson vs. Tilden and Johnston. On the opening day Brookes, now more than fifteen years older than the day he came to England for his "go" at Laurie Doherty, met the new champion of the Western world. He was too old to learn new tricks but his old ones brought him within a point of the first set. Brookes was always striving for the net position while Tilden remained back for the most part. It was volley against drive. After Brookes reached set point at 5-3 Tilden recovered and won the set at 10-8. He then took Brookes' service in the tenth game for the second set at 6-4. In the third set Brookes changed his tactics and, after losing the first game, won six in a row for the set at 6-1. After the rest he went to 3-0 in the fourth set, making a run of nine straight games. Tilden won the next five games before Brookes got the ninth. Tilden served out the match for 6-4.

The Johnston-Patterson match found Johnston at the top of his form and Patterson at his worst. Everything the Australian tried went wrong. None of his first serves went in. His drives were wild and his whole game went to pieces. Patterson won only five games in the three sets and was quite outclassed.

The Cup was won the following day when Tilden and Johnston defeated Brookes and Patterson three sets to one. The Americans lost the first set 6-4, then improved their teamwork and took advantage of the Australians' lapses. Brookes felt the effect of his singles match the previous day. He made eleven errors in the first set to Patterson's two. The next three sets went to the Americans at 6-4, 6-0, 6-4. At its conclusion the gallery rose and cheered both teams.

In spite of the fact that the tie was now over, the final singles were played and brought out some of the best tennis of the tie. Brookes was magnificent against Johnston. He won the first set 7-5 and led 5-2 in the second. But Johnston was wearing the veteran down, ran five games for the set and the next two 6-3, 6-3. In the final contest, Patterson took the first set 7-5 but Tilden's accuracy and hard hitting proved too much for the Australian and Tilden took the next three sets, 6-2, 6-3, 6-3. The Cup was ready to be returned to the United States for a long stay.

9

Attack on America

When Tilden and Johnston won the Cup from Australasia in 1920, a new era in the game of Lawn Tennis commenced. Not only had the supremacy of the two Bills been established but a change of scene after seven years brought about larger entries and many new nations into the competition.

When the draw for the 1921 contest was made there were twelve challengers, five more than the largest previous entry in 1913. Seven nations which had never competed before joined the lists – Argentina, Czechoslovakia, Denmark, India, Japan, the Philippines and Spain. They were joined by Australasia, Belgium, the British Isles, Canada and France. Argentina and Denmark drew byes in the upper half and India and France in the lower. The British Isles vs. Spain, Belgium vs. Phillipines completed the draw. Three of these ties were played in Europe; the rest were held in the U. S.

The tie between the British Isles and Spain was played at Hendon, near London, on May 23, 24 and 25. A controversy arose when Randolph Lycett was named to the British side. Although he was born in England, Lycett had played most of his tennis in Australia. F. G. Lowe played singles with Lycett, and Lycett and Max Woosnam were the doubles team. Spain named her two ranking players, Count Manuel de Gomar and Manuel Alonso. On the first day Lowe beat de Gomar in four sets and Lycett beat Alonso in three. When the doubles was won on the second day, the British had won the tie, but Spain avoided a shut-out when Alonso beat Lowe 8-6, 6-1, 8-6.

Belgium met Czechoslovakia at Prague June 13, 15 and 16 and won by three matches to two. Jean Washer and M. Lammens played all five matches for Belgium. Ladislav Zemla and K. Ardelt were named for the singles by the Czechs. J. Just joined Zemla in the doubles. Zemla won both his matches and so the result depended on the doubles, which went to the fifth set before the Belgians prevailed. The Philippines defaulted to give Japan a walk-over into the second round. Argentina also defaulted to

Denmark in a second round tie, as did Belgium to Japan.

So far Tilden's major triumphs had all been won on grass. He now wanted to prove that varying court surfaces are only a means of adaptation of fundamental principles. The World's Hard Court Championship at Paris gave Tilden the opportunity he wanted. He lost only three sets on his way to the final, where he beat Jean Washer. A week later he was in a London hospital. He was not released until the second week of Wimbledon was well under way. Luckily it was the last year in which the holder stood out to meet the winner of the all-comers' in the challenge round. Even so, Tilden was a sick man when he faced Brian Norton of South Africa with only four days' light practice to put him on edge. He gave a pathetic exhibition. He could do nothing right. Norton had two sets in his pocket in less than half an hour. With victory in sight Norton eased up. Tilden won the third set but Norton reached match point in the fourth. Tilden, with a desperate effort, placed a drop shot out of Norton's reach. A spectator cried, "Play the game, Tilden." The incident upset Norton's concentration. Tilden seized the opportunity and carried off the victory.

The last tie of the year played in Europe brought together India and France at Paris July 16, 17 and 18. William Laurentz and Jean Samazeuilh, the new French champion, played the opening singles for France, with Jacques Brugnon joining Laurentz in the doubles. S. M. Jacob and Mohamed Sleem were named by India for the singles, with L. S. Deane and A. A. Fyzee for the doubles. India scored an upset by winning the tie, 4-1.

In the opening match Samazeulh beat Jacob in straight sets, but Sleem evened the score with a five set win over Laurentz. The doubles went to the Indians, also in five sets. Sleem overpowered Samazeuilh 6-1, 6-3, 6-3 after an interruption by rain. With the tie won, Brugnon and Deane substituted in the fifth match which again went to five sets with Deane taking the fifth at 8-6.

Play now moved to North America with Australasia meeting Canada at Toronto July 23, 26 and 27. It was Canada's first match at home, and Henri Laframboise, Paul Bennett and George Holmes were selected to do the honors for the home side. Patterson and Brookes were not available and Australasia sent J. O. Anderson, John B. Hawkes and Clarence Todd under the captaincy of Norman Peach. Australasia won by five rubbers to none.

Hawkes beat Bennett in the first match in three close sets. Both men were new to Davis Cup play. Hawkes played a steady, cautious game while Bennett knew nothing but to go to the net on every occasion, despite the risks. The Anderson-Laframboise match was quite different. Laframboise was a fine volleyer and made few mistakes in winning the first set 6-4. Anderson just saved the second at 7-5, and after that the rest was easy. He became more aggressive and took the third and fourth sets 6-0, 6-2.

The doubles was rained out for two days and eventually played on an en-tout-cas court instead of on grass. Anderson and Todd were both big men and hard hitters: Bennett and Holmes, an experienced pair, were no match for them. The scores were 6-2, 6-3, 6-1, giving the Australasians the tie. On the third day Todd was substituted for Hawkes and beat Laframboise in four sets. Against Bennett, in the fifth match, Anderson lost only five games.

The scene now shifted to the Allegheny Country Club near Pittsburgh, where the famous tie between the Germans and Australasians had been held in 1914. Again an Australasian team was a competitor and their opponents were the British team, composed of Max Woosnam, F. G. Lowe, O. G. N. Turnbull and J. Brian Gilbert. The weather was bad, rain following the Australasians from Toronto and interfering with the practice of both teams at Sewickley. This was particularly hard on the Englishmen who had only recently come off shipboard.

Anderson and Woosnam met in the first match. Woosnam, a small man, appeared even smaller compared with the giant stature of Anderson, yet he started quickly and carried the first set to 6-4 before Anderson settled down. The next two sets also went to the tall Australian, 6-2, 6-4. Lowe evened the count by beating Hawkes in straight sets, his stonewall defense putting Hawkes at a complete disadvantage. Anderson and Todd beat Woosnam and Turnbull in the doubles in five sets, the loss of Woosnam's service at 3-all in the fifth being the turning point. On the final day, Anderson won the tie with his defeat of Lowe in four sets. Woosnam accounted for another British victory when he beat Hawkes after the Aussie led two sets to one.

Two weeks later the two semi-final ties were played. Australasia met Denmark at the Mayfield Country Club in Cleveland, while Japan and India faced each other at the Onwentsia Club at Chicago. Both ties were played on grass.

The Danish team was composed of Vagn Ingerslev, the Danish champion, Erik Tegner and Paul Henriksen. For Australasia, Captain Peach took Hawkes' place in singles. The result was a 5-0 win for Australasia. The only sets they lost were when Ingerslev won the first and fourth from Peach.

At Chicago, India fielded the same three-man team which had defeated France, while Japan placed its fortunes entirely in the hands of Zenzo Shimizu and Ichiya Kumagae. Kumagae was a graduate of Keio University, had lived in the United States for several years and had a place in the American ranking since 1916. He was a left-hander with a completely self-taught style. Yet he was so persistent and so eager to improve that he made his mark. Shimizu had been Tilden's opponent in the All-Comers' final at Wimbledon in 1920 and, though his strokes were awkward, was a more finished player than his compatriot. Both were well-accustomed to grass, a great disadvantage to their opponents. Only three sets were lost by the Japanese on the way to a 5-0 win. Fyzee took the first set from Kumagae and he and Deane won the third and fourth sets of the doubles.

The historic Casino at Newport was the venue of the final between Australasia and Japan. The Japanese created something of a sensation by winning 4 matches to 1, gaining the challenge round for Japan's first and only time.

Shimizu and Anderson met in the opening match and Shimizu's crafty play had Anderson floundering from the first. He was the more resourceful and the steadier of the two. His service was kept low and he made very few errors. The scores were 6-4, 7-5, 6-4.

Hawkes started like a winner against Kumagae. He won the first two sets by aggressive play and hard hitting and went to 3-2, 40-0 in the third. At that point a strange transformation took place. Kumagae found his game and began to force matters. Hawkes was taken aback but recovered and reached 5-4. Then he eased instead of pressing on and missed several opportunities to win the set. Kumagae eventually won it at 8-6 and took the next two 6-2, 6-3. The doubles went to four sets, with Anderson and Todd the winners after the Japanese won the first set. On the final day, Anderson opened against Kumagae and again wasted his opportunities. He won the first and third sets but could not maintain a high level and persisted in changing a winning game. Kumagae saw his opening in the fourth and made the most of it, losing only two games in the last set. Hawkes won the first from Shimizu but was helpless thereafter.

The Challenge Round was played at the West Side Club in Forest Hills on September 2, 3 and 5. Stands seating 12,000 had been erected, and although the tie had been won on the second day, more than 14,000 turned out on Labor Day to see the concluding matches. Johnston beat Kumagae easily in the first match, 6-2, 6-4, 6-2. Kumagae was off his game and Johnston had little opposition.

Tilden had not entirely recovered from his illness in London but somewhat underrated Shimizu and started with the intention of playing from the baseline. He led 3-0 before Shimizu reached his best form. Playing chiefly from backcourt he drove hard and accurately. His service was kept low with a lot of spin and beautifully placed. Tilden reached 5-3, but Shimizu took the first set 7-5. At four-all in the second set Tilden began to go to the net, was passed clean and lost his service. Shimizu ran out the set 6-4. Again in the third Tilden reached 4-2, but Shimizu made almost miraculous recoveries, broke Tilden in the ninth and got to 30-0 with only two points for the match. He lost the game but again got to 40-15 on Tilden's service. Again Tilden pulled out of danger and finally won the set 7-5.

It was a hot, humid day and both players were on the verge of exhaustion. When play was resumed after the interval, Tilden had recuperated but Shimizu suffered from cramps and was even worse off than when he had left the court. Tilden raced through the next two sets with the loss of only three games.

The United States now led two rubbers to none. Williams and Washburn put the finishing touches on the tie with a win at 6-2, 7-5, 4-6, 7-5. Kumagae faced Tilden in the first match on the third day. He was in poor health and was playing his last big match. Tilden was much improved over his showing against Shimizu. Kumagae resisted in the first set, which Tilden won 9-7. The last two sets went to "Big Bill", 6-4, 6-1. In the final match, Shimizu played as strongly against Johnston as he had against Tilden, winning the second set 7-5 and turning Johnston's fastest forehands for clean passes. But the Japanese had no further resources to match Johnston's controlled speed and when he lost the third set 6-2, he put up only a feeble resistance in the fourth. He had given of his best and it was not quite good enough.

IO

A New Challenger

Two more challengers entered the lists in 1922. Three of these were newcomers – Roumania, Italy and Hawaii – but because of difficulties in completing representative teams and the long distances to be traveled, there were four defaults in the first round. Canada was drawn to play France in Europe, but the June date was too early for the Canadian players to get in shape. Kumagae had returned to Japan and there was no one available to replace him. Hawaii and the Philippines were unable to meet the cost of sending teams to Europe. This left only two first round ties and both were played in England.

Roumania met India at Beckenham and lost 5-0. The two Fyzees were India's singles players and C. Ramaswami teamed with A. H. Fyzee in doubles. Nicolas Mishu and Michael Stern represented Roumania. Mishu won the first two sets from A. A. Fyzee but lost the next three, the fifth at love. Again, against A. H. Fyzee, Mishu won the first set but lost the next three. The doubles went to the Indians in straight sets.

Australasia defeated Belgium at Scarborough June 22 to 24 by 4 rubbers to 0, the final singles not being played. Patterson and Anderson won their three singles against Washer and A. G. Watson without the loss of a set. Pat O'Hara Wood teamed with Anderson in the doubles and the match went to five sets, with the score 6-1, 6-2, 4-6, 7-9, 7-5.

Three of the four second round matches were also played in England. Alonso and de Gomar won their four singles against the Fyzee brothers but, with Eduardo Flaquer teaming with de Gomar in the doubles, Spain lost the match, leaving the score 4-1. The British Isles defeated Italy 4-0 at Roehampton June 19-21. Cesare Colombo and Balbi Robecco played all five matches for Italy but did not win a set from Kingscote, Lowe and Frank Riseley. Kingscote defaulted to Robecco in the final match. Australasia won from Czechoslovakia July 14 and 15 at Roehampton, 5-0. Dohrer and Ardelt played all five rubbers for the Czechs. For the Australasians Anderson and Patterson played the singles, while Patterson and R. C. Wertheim teamed in doubles.

The fourth tie between France and Denmark was played at Copenhagen June 17-19, with France winning 4-1. The only Danish point came when Ingerslev beat the French substitute, Jean Couiteas, in the last rubber. This tie was especially notable for the first appearance on the French team of two young players, Jean Borotra and Henri Cochet. A year earlier (in the 1921 Covered Court Criterium) they met in the final, with Cochet the winner. They were totally unknown to each other and to the officials before their opening matches, and the contrast in their personalities and styles did not fail to impress that Parisian gathering.

Borotra was a Basque lad of twenty-two who had come to Paris to enter the Ecole Polytechnique. He had not played more than two matches before he won the affection of the gallery. He dashed for the net on every occasion, for his service was labored and his ground strokes unorthodox. He planted himself in forecourt and volleyed with a brio and good humor which won him instant acclaim.

Across the net was a typical city-bred "gamin," a short, tough, self-confident boy who amazed the onlookers by his mastery of the most difficult strokes. Cochet was brought up within a stone's throw of one of Lyons' best indoor courts. He had a racket in his hand at five. As he grew to a point where he could look over and not through the net, he began to consider it a factor to be reckoned with. Young as he was, he considered victory more important than style.

When Spain won from British Isles by default, the only remaining semi-final tie was between Australasia and France. At Wimbledon Patterson had regained his title: he beat Borotra in an early round, Anderson in the semi-final and Lycett in the final. The challenge Round had been abolished and neither Tilden nor any of the Americans came over to London. Anderson accompanied Patterson and Wood to America to meet the French at Longwood August 10-14. Shortly after their arrival, Anderson was confined to a hospital with pneumonia.

As France prepared to send its first team overseas, Cochet was in the Army and Samazeuilh was selected in his place, along with Borotra and Gobert. But Cochet prevailed upon his Colonel to let him go and he arrived at the Federation office just as Samazeuilh was getting into a taxi on the way to the station. The luckless substitute climbed out, helped Cochet into his place and waved good-bye to his mates.

The Captain of the team was Allan Muhr, an American who had come to France before the war at a time when all forms of sport in France were undeveloped. The officials thought that his origin and knowledge of the language would be invaluable on this American trip. Before the team reached Boston, Muhr had already made up his mind to name Gobert and Cochet to carry the entire burden. Even though Borotra proved in practice that he was better on grass than Cochet, Muhr stuck to his plan.

During the first part of the Gobert-Patterson match it seemed as though he had made the right choice. Gobert won the first two sets but now Patterson changed his tactics and took the net more often. Gobert got upset and lost his concentration. He was disturbed at the footing. He did not like the bound of the ball. Patterson won the third set and, after Gobert had a 3-0 lead in the fourth, ran five games in a row and took that one too. Gobert was cooked, fell, got cramps in his racket hand, footfaulted and lost the match.

Cochet justified his selection by beating Wood in five sets to even the tie. A last minute change by Muhr might yet have saved the day. Cochet and Borotra had played doubles continuously together for two years. Gobert had never played with either. Yet Gobert and Cochet were named to oppose the team which had been runners-up at Wimbledon. The teamwork of the Australasians was more effective than the individual and spasmodic brilliance of the Frenchmen. Cochet rose to great heights in the last two sets but Gobert weakened, fell, and lost heart. Australasia had the vital point by the score of 6-0, 6-8, 4-6, 6-3, 10-8. When Wood beat Gobert on the last day the tie was over.

Spain and Australasia met in the final on August 17-19 at Germantown. Manuel Alonso and de Gomar played for Spain, with Jose Alonso as Captain. Patterson and Wood represented Australasia. The result was another 4-1 win for the men from Down Under, Spain's only point coming when Alonso beat Wood in five sets on the opening day. An unusual incident occurred during this match. Wood won the first two sets and was leading in the fourth at 5-2, 40-30, match point. On his second service Wood crashed a cannonball straight down the center line which Alonso could not reach. But his foot swung over the line and a foot-fault was called. Both players came to the net to shake hands believing the match was over, but they were called back. Alonso pulled up, won the set at 8-6 and the fifth at 6-1.

During the three weeks which followed, Anderson had recovered from his bout of pneumonia and replaced Wood in the singles when the team met the defending American champions at Forest Hills on September 1, 2 and 5. Vincent Richards had teamed with Tilden to win his third doubles championship from the Patterson-Wood combination and was selected for the doubles. Tilden and Johnston played the singles. Tilden met Patterson in the first match and the Australian forced him to 7-5, 10-8 in the first two sets. In the third set Tilden let loose and won six games in a row.

When Anderson faced Johnston, it was soon seen that he was far from himself. Little Bill was devastating, played almost entirely from backcourt and won 6-1, 6-2, 6-3. The doubles was a complete turnabout from the result at Longwood: the Australians lost only seven games in the three sets they needed to win. Johnston's defeat of Patterson 6-2, 6-2, 6-1 on the third day clinched the tie. The Tilden-Anderson match which followed, though nothing depended on the outcome, went to five sets, with Anderson showing much of his former form.

The constant increase in the number of challengers – they rose to 17 in 1923 – led to the adoption of the Zone system that year. Thirteen nations were drawn in the European Zone and four in the American. This necessitated an earlier start for the first round and, at Bordeaux on May 15-17, France defeated Denmark 4-1. Cochet and Samazeuilh represented France with a new player, Rene Lacoste, on the team for the first time. His debut was not auspicious as he lost his match with Larsen for the only Danish win.

Six years Borotra's junior and three years younger than Cochet, Lacoste never saw a tennis court until he visited England in 1919. He was not content to analyze the tactics he had failed to master. He studied the methods of other players, weeded out the mediocre and set to perfecting what was sound.

In other first round matches Great Britain beat Belgium 3-2; Switzerland beat Czechoslovakia by the same score, Ireland did likewise with India, and Spain beat Roumania by default. Among the new players who appeared that year were L. A. Godfree of Great Britain, Charles Aeschliman of Switzerland and Umberto Morpurgo of Italy.

In the second round, France dropped Lacoste in singles but paired him with Brugnon in doubles. Ireland was beaten at Dublin 4-1, Holland beat Italy at Noordwijk 5-0, Switzerland beat Argentina at Geneva 4-1, and Spain beat Great Britain at Manchester 3-2.

The Americans returned to Wimbledon in force with Johnston, Richards and Hunter in the van. Johnston had won the French championship and lost only one set at Wimbledon where he beat Hunter in the final. Following this, Spain defeated Holland 5-0 in one semi-final while France, with Blanchy, Cochet and Samazeulh, squeaked through against Switzerland 3-2 in the other. In the European Zone final, played at Deauville the end of July, Blanchy and Lacoste were the singles players, with Cochet and Brugnon teaming in the doubles. Again the score was a tenuous 3-2.

In the American Zone, Japan, with Fukuda and Kashio assisting Shimizu, defeated Canada at Montreal 5-0. The same week-end at Orange,

Australasia, with Anderson and Hawkes, beat Hawaii 4-1. The final was played at Chicago August 9-12 and the Australians triumphed by 4 to 1.

Australasia met a weakened French team at Longwood August 16-18 and lost only one match when Lacoste beat the Australasian substitute, McInnes, in the last singles. Borotra and Cochet pleaded business interests to avoid another fruitless trip to America, and Pierre Hirsch and Brugnon were named along with Lacoste.

In the Challenge Round at Forest Hills August 31 to September 3, Johnston suffered his first Davis Cup defeat when he lost to Anderson in five sets. Tilden won both his matches and Johnston recovered to beat Hawkes 6-0, 6-2, 6-1. The doubles was the crucial match of the tie. Tilden and Richards had broken up their partnership, and Dick Williams was named to support Big Bill in the Challenge Round. Both were left court players and it was decided that Tilden should take the right court. It was not a happy partnership. After winning the first set 17-15, the Americans lost the second 13-11 and the third 6-2. There were recriminations in the dressing room and Tilden went back determined to win. Williams, too, worked miracles and the last two sets went to United States 6-3, 6-2.

Again in 1924 there was a record entry of 23 nations. Seventeen of these elected to play in the European Zone and six in the American Zone.

The French officials recognized that the elements of victory were at hand. All that was necessary was to combine them into a team which would establish France as the champion nation. It was quite by chance that the first step was taken. Ever since they came to the front, Borotra and Cochet had paired in doubles. It was never a happy combination. Now Borotra found an ideal partner in Lacoste, while Brugnon's steadiness complemented Cochet's weaknesses. Borotra could now devote himself to his ambitions in singles.

His first success was in the French Championships. Lacoste helped him by putting out Cochet in the semi-final. Wimbledon was the next goal. Although he was French Champion, Borotra was by no means favored to win. There were the Americans, Richards, Hunter, Washburn and Williams. There was the Belgian, Washer, and the Englishman, Kingscote. There was also the 47-year-old Norman Brookes, who beat Hunter in the third round. Borotra beat Richards, Lacoste accounted for Washer and Williams. The two Frenchmen met in the final in one of the shortest five-set matches on record, with Borotra beating Lacoste.

The Olympic Games at Paris followed. Borotra's Wimbledon honors did not suffice to shake off the Cochet spell. Richards won the title after beating both Cochet and Lacoste.

In Davis Cup play, France again experimented with tried and untried combinations and yet came to the final after defeating Ireland 5-0, India 4-0 and Great Britain 4-1. It was in this match that the final combination first made its appearance, with Cochet and Lacoste playing the singles and Borotra and Brugnon the doubles. Great Britain had come through to the semi-final by defeating Belgium, Spain and South Africa. The other finalist was Czechoslovakia, with Zemla and Rohrer in the singles and Zemla and Jan Kozeluh for the doubles. The Czechs had beaten New Zealand (a new entry), Switzerland and Denmark. The result was a 5-0 win for France and another trip to America.

In the American Zone, Canada beat Cuba in the first round but lost to Japan in the semi-final. Australia (no longer Australasia) beat China and Mexico and then Japan in the final, all by 5-0 scores. Patterson and Wood were the Australian team and, in the Interzone final, played at Longwood September 4-6, Lacoste and Borotra played the singles while Lacoste teamed with Brugnon in the doubles. Lacoste set down both Patterson and Wood. If only Borotra had been able to defeat one of them, the French would have been in the Challenge Round. But the staleness which had marked his play since Wimbledon still had him in its grip. After Wood beat him on the first day, he made such a miserable showing against Patterson that the Australian dubbed him an honorary member of his team.

Richards' successes abroad and his win over Johnston in the East-West matches won him the second singles position on the defending Davis Cup team. The Challenge Round was the most impressive victory for United States since they won the Cup in 1920. All four singles matches were won without the loss of a set, and Tilden and Johnston won the doubles in four.

It was to be twelve years before an Australian team was again in the Challenge Round. Over the horizon loomed a new challenger which, after two unsuccessful attempts, won the Cup as the fourth nation to hold it in its long history.

II

The "Musketeers" Carry Off the Cup

Borotra's win over Lacoste at Wimbledon in 1924 convinced the officials of the French Federation that they were at last on the way. To make sure of ultimate success they abandoned the fallacy that they needed an ex-American as Captain and appointed their great former Champion, Max Decugis, to direct the destinies of the team. Their judgment was proved to be correct at the start of 1925.

Lacoste won the Coupe de Noel and the French Covered Court Championship. Borotra, on a business trip to the United States, won the American Indoor Championship. Lacoste won the French Championship in the spring and teamed with Borotra to win the doubles. At Wimbledon the three Frenchmen, Borotra, Cochet and Lacoste, beat Anderson. In a repeat of their 1924 meeting Lacoste turned the tables on his compatriot, 6-3, 6-3, 4-6, 8-6.

Meanwhile the preliminary rounds of the Davis Cup contest were being played. Once more the entries topped the previous year's, reaching the record of 25, of which 16 challenged in the European Zone and 9 in the American. Bars against former enemy nations were further relaxed, and Hungary and Austria entered the lists, along with Sweden, Portugal and Poland. Borotra, Lacoste and Brugnon were the mainstays of the French team, with Paul Feret as substitute. They went through four rounds with the loss of only one rubber, when Bela Kehrling of Hungary beat Borotra at Budapest on May 8. Italy, represented by de Morpurgo and Colombo; Great Britain, with O. G. N. Turnbull as its No. 1; and Holland, with Timmer, Kool and van Lennep, were France's other victims.

Close 3-2 ties in the first round brought victories by Holland over Czechoslovakia, both Macenauer and Kozeluh beating Kool; Sweden over Switzerland, and India over Belgium. Austria beat Ireland, Italy beat Portugal and Denmark beat Roumania, all by 4-1 scores. Great Britain did not lose a set in defeating Poland. All the second round ties were shut-outs, with Great Britain defeating Denmark, Holland over Sweden, India over

Austria, and France over Italy.

In the semi-finals Holland beat India 4-1, A. H. Fyzee's win over van Lennep being India's only victory, and France ran through Great Britain 4-0, the last singles being abandoned. In the final, played at Noordwijk on July 18-20, Lacoste and Borotra took three singles from Timmer and Kool, and Lacoste and Brugnon won the doubles in four sets.

In the American Zone, Spain beat Cuba at Havana 5-0 and followed with another 5-0 win over Mexico. The other second round ties went by default to Japan over China, Australia over Hawaii, and Canada over New Zealand. With Harada and Shimizu playing all five matches, Japan defeated Spain, with two Alonsos and Flaquer, by 3 rubbers to 2. Shimizu, a shadow of his former self, was beaten in both his matches, but the win of the doubles gave the Japanese the tie. In the other half, Anderson and Patterson, with Hawkes in doubles, beat Crocker and Wright of Canada 5-0. In the American Zone final, played at Longwood on August 20-22, Australia qualified for the Interzone final by defeating Japan 4-1. The surprise of this tie was Harada's four set win over Patterson.

France and Australia met in the Interzone final at Forest Hills on September 4, 5 and 7, with the Challenge Round scheduled for Germantown a week later. Captain Decugis named Lacoste and Borotra for all five matches, while the Australians used their tried singles players, Patterson and Anderson, and their premier doubles team of Patterson and Hawkes. Patterson was the dominating figure from start to finish and won 6-3, 6-4, 6-2. Another surprise was in store when Borotra took the court against Anderson. The Borotra of 1924 who had fizzled so ingloriously was no more, and his opponent was no more the Anderson of 1923. France evened the score by 6-4,6-3, 8-6.

The doubles match on Saturday was full of both good and bad tennis, with plenty of thrills. Borotra was the outstanding star. He did not slump at any time and carried Lacoste for long stretches. For the Australians, Hawkes had nothing but his service, while Patterson was unsteady at several crucial periods. France won the first and third sets, Australia the second and fourth. In the fifth France went into the lead at 5-2. Hawkes was serving and three times he was caught by a ball at his feet and France had two match points. But Australia won four points and the game. With Lacoste serving, France had another match point but lost it, and Patterson's service made the score 5-all. To 8-all it was even, all four men playing at their best. Lacoste was steady as a rock and brought the score to 9-8. Hawkes again faltered and, though the Australians saved two more match points, the French came through for a win at 10-8.

The weather turned bad on Sunday, with rain all day continuing into the night. There seemed little prospect of concluding the tie on Monday, which was the Labor Day holiday. A scattering of spectators was in the stands when it was decided to go ahead. The tarpaulins were removed and Patterson and Borotra commenced the match on which all depended. Patterson played the best game he had shown in America since 1922. He won the first set 6-4 and, after Patterson won the opening of the third, Borotra responded with a run of six games for the set at 6-1. Games followed service to 3-all in the fourth set and when Patterson dropped his service, Borotra went all out and took the deciding game for a 6-3 win. The uncertain weather compelled abandonment of the final match, but France was already in the Challenge Round for the first time.

Their hopes encouraged by this victory, the French team went into the match against the United States with great confidence. Tilden and Johnston were there to oppose them, with Richards and Williams in the doubles. Though Tilden was down one set to two against Borotra and two sets to none to Lacoste, he pulled out both matches in the fifth set. Johnston lost the third set to Lacoste but beat Borotra 6-1, 6-4, 6-0. The doubles was also a straight set win for the Americans. The failure to win a match did not seem so important to Captain Decugis as the fact that both Borotra and Lacoste had carried the great Tilden to the limit. When he landed at Cherbourg, the French Captain said: "The Davis Cup will be ours before 1930. Tilden is still in a class by himself but he is past thirty. So is Johnston. Cochet and Lacoste are nearer twenty than thirty. They will and must improve."

The events of 1926 proved his words to have been prophetic. Lacoste, Borotra and Brugnon came to the United States in February and swept all before them in the Indoor Championships. Lacoste won the singles, with Borotra the runner-up, and in a team match which followed, Lacoste beat both Tilden and Richards in straight sets. Cochet was married early in the year and began to interest himself seriously in tennis. He won the French Championship by beating Washer, Richards and Lacoste in turn. Lacoste's doctor forbade him to play at Wimbledon. Borotra again proved he was a better man than Cochet on grass and won his second All-England title. Cochet and Brugnon won the doubles from Richards and Howard Kinsey.

For the first time since the early days, Australia did not challenge for the Davis Cup and the field was reduced to 24, 19 in the European Zone and 5 in the American. Japan, playing Harada and Tawara, beat Mexico 4-1 and Philippines 5-0. Cuba beat Canada 3-2 and Japan won the final 5-0.

To captain the French Davis Cup team, the Federation chose Pierre Gillou, whose record as a player was inferior to that of Decugis but whose capacity as a strategist and administrator could not be equalled. Lacoste,

Cochet and Brugnon played the first tie against Denmark and won 5-0. Three rubbers were all that were needed to conquer the Czechoslovakian team of Kozeluh, Macenauer and Zelma. Borotra replaced Lacoste for the semi-final against Sweden, another 5-0 win, and all four, assisted by Pierre Landry, won the European Zone final at Cabourg July 24-26 against the British team of Gregory, Turnbull, Crole-Rees and Kingsley. At a dinner shortly after their arrival in America, Henry Slocum christened them "The Musketeers."

In the opening match against Japan, Cochet stood two sets down to Tawara. Gillou feared for the outcome. "Well, Henri?" he asked. "All right," Cochet replied. "It takes a little time." He did win in the fifth set but Harada beat Lacoste to even the score. Gillou took no chances in the doubles and named the Wimbledon Champions. They lost only two games. Lacoste beat Tawara to win the tie, but Cochet lost to Harada in the final rubber.

In the Challenge Round the American team of Johnston, Tilden, Williams and Richards wiped up the court in the first four matches. Johnston beat Lacoste by the peculiar score of 6-0, 6-4, 0-6, 6-0. Tilden beat Borotra in straight sets, and Cochet and Brugnon lost the doubles. On the third day Johnston continued the rout with a three set win over Borotra and then, to everyone's surprise, Lacoste took Tilden's measure 4-6, 6-4, 8-6, 8-6. In the thirteenth game of the third set, Tilden slipped a cartilage in his left knee and Lacoste broke his serve and won the set. Tilden played through the fourth set on nerve, but he could not run and Lacoste had the match. It was Tilden's first singles loss in Davis Cup play, but worse was yet to come.

Gillou had already sailed for home when the Championships commenced at Forest Hills. He was disgusted with the showing of his men. Yet all four Frenchmen reached the quarter-final. There Brugnon lost to Richards, Borotra beat Johnston, Lacoste beat Williams, and Cochet beat Tilden at 8-6 in the fifth set. Borotra beat Richards in one semi-final while Lacoste beat Cochet in the other. In the final Borotra called upon every strategical resource to beat his calm and machine-like compatriot. Lacoste knew better than to waste sympathy on a man who was only waiting for the slightest slackening to leap to the attack. Rene took the title in straight sets.

All three Frenchmen had now beaten Tilden. Resolved on revenge, he went to Europe to see if he could repeat his triumphs of 1921. At St. Cloud he beat Cochet and met Lacoste in the final. The match lasted three and one-half hours. The fifth set went to twenty games. The end came when Tilden served a double-fault. Wimbledon was even more sensational. Borotra went all out to win from Lacoste. Tilden, against Cochet, stood at two sets to love and 5-1 in the third. Tilden served two aces and was only two points from victory. Then a complete form reversal took place. Cochet won seventeen straight points and got himself back in the battle. Tilden had leads in the fourth and fifth sets but Cochet won them both. In the final against Borotra, Cochet lost the first two sets for the third successive time. Again he rallied but Borotra reached match point in the fifth. He missed an easy volley. Four more times he stood within a stroke of victory. Each time Cochet pulled it out. In the twelfth game the title was his.

Twenty-five nations challenged for the Davis Cup that year, only four of which entered the American Zone. Australis was again an absentee and Japan, with Harada and Ohta for the singles and Toba alternating with Shimizu in the doubles, beat Mexico 4-1 and Canada (which had defeated Cuba) by three rubbers to two. Gillou, playing his cards skillfully so as to bring his men to their peak for the Challenge Round was unconcerned about 5-0 wins. Nevertheless, France had a comparatively easy road to the European Zone final. Roumania was beaten 4-1 in the second round, Italy 3-2 in the third and South Africa 5-0 in the semi-final. In the final at Copenhagen July 21-22 against Denmark, Einar Ulrich and Axel Peterson were defeated 3-0, the last two singles being unplayed.

France met Japan at Longwood August 25-27 and again only three matches were played. Cochet and Lacoste beat Harada and Ohta in the singles, and Brugnon and Cochet defeated Toba-Harada in the doubles, all without the loss of a set. The French team commenced to prepare for the Challenge Round.

Cochet, confident and lazy, took only a short work-out each day. Borotra and Brugnon gave each other light exercise. Lacoste's method was all his own. He kept the strictest training regime. He spent his evenings studying his casebook. He imprinted on his mind the strokes and tactics of Tilden and Johnston. In the morning he worked out his reply on the court. When he met Johnston in the first match at Germantown on September 8, he knew exactly what he must do. Johnston won only seven games. Now it was up to Cochet to repeat his Wimbledon victory over Tilden. His preparation had been negligent. Tilden was fighting on his home ground. Cochet won only the second set.

The American officials had difficulty selecting their doubles team. Richards had become a professional. Williams and Tilden were both left-court players. Johnston did not care to play doubles. The choice finally fell on Tilden and Hunter, who had won at Wimbledon. Gillou gambled and chose Borotra and Brugnon. It was a wise choice. His two single players had a day of rest while Tilden was near the end of his resources when he and Hunter had to go to five sets to beat the Frenchmen.

With only one out of the two remaining singles to be won, it seemed as though the United States might come through. But Lacoste repeated his 1926 win over Tilden, this time in four sets. The score was tied. Everything hung on the last match between Cochet and Johnston.

The first two sets were divided. Then Cochet won the third. It was plain that Johnston had lost some of the skill which for six years had enabled him to win by such overpowering scores. When Cochet reached 5-2 in the fourth set, Johnston's admirers were prepared to see him die in beauty. But the little man was not yet done. After deuce had been called eight times, he won the eighth game. Then he took Cochet's service at love. Cochet was worried. If he had been left to his own devices he might have given up the fight. But Lacoste was sitting at the courtside. He called Cochet to him, told him the strokes to play and gave him renewed courage. He followed Lacoste's advice. He forced Johnston into error and won the match. The Davis Cup was handed over to France.

In the Championship Lacoste proved himself to be the greatest of the Frenchmen. Hennessey beat an erratic Cochet. Borotra lost to Tilden. Lacoste took on the two Bills, one after the other, and held his title for another year.

The trip home was one continuous celebration. France was on top of the tennis world. She held her own, the English and the American titles. She was also the Champion Nation. Champagne flowed all day and all night. Cochet and Brugnon and Borotra and Captain Gillou responded to toast after toast. Lacoste, with his serious smile, paid his share of the bottles and retired early to his cabin. He was already planning the defense of the Cup.

12

Tilden Reaches the End of the Road

France was the Champion Nation and intended to hold the Cup for a long time – even longer, if possible, than the American run of seven years between 1920 and 1926. This required organization and experience. As the Challenge Round would now be played in Paris at the height of the European season, the whole schedule was rearranged. The first round in the European Zone was set for the first week in May with the second round to be completed during the following two weeks. The French Championships were to be played during the last week of May, the third and fourth rounds followed, and there was another intermission for Wimbledon. The European Zone final was scheduled for July 13-15, the Interzone final for July 20-22 and the Challenge Round for July 27-30. The American Zone ties commenced in April and were concluded the first week in June.

To do honor to the 32 nations which entered – by far the largest to date–as well as to provide a fitting setting for their Championships, the Federation sought the help of the Stade Français and the Racing Club, which had held previous championships on their grounds at St. Cloud and the Croix Catelan, and obtained a subsidy from the Government. They selected a site at Auteuil, just outside Paris, to be named Stade Roland Garros after a French tennis player and aviator who was killed in the War. A center court and four outside courts of En-tout-Cas were constructed and the center court was surrounded by a wooden stand seating 10,000.

Most of the European nations which had taken part in previous years were in the lists, and New Zealand, Australia, Chile, Argentina and the Philippines joined them. Australia's team included Gerald Patterson and two young players whose names became well-known in later years – Jack Crawford and Harry Hopman. They had the misfortune to meet Italy at Genoa in the first round and lost 4-1. Austria beat the Philippines, England beat Argentina and Spain beat Chile. New Zealand drew a bye and beat Portugal in the second round before losing to Czechoslovakia.

Germany's team included Froitzheim and Kleinschroth from pre-war days, with Moldenhauer and Prenn representing the new generation. England relied on Gregory and Higgs of the 1927 team, with Crole-Rees and Eames in the doubles. Kozeluh and Macenauer, aided by a newcomer, Roderich Menzel, played for the Czechs, and Timmer and van Lennep carried the flag for Holland. In the semi-finals Italy defeated England at Felixstowe 4-1, while the Czechs beat Holland at Prague 3-2. In the final, played at Milan, di Morpurgo beat both Kozeluh and Macenauer. Gaslini defeated Macenauer but lost to Kozeluh and the Czechs won the doubles, making the final score for Italy 3-2.

For the United States, Billy Johnston had retired and Bill Tilden was left to fight alone with a group of younger players. In the American Zone first round, Japan beat Cuba and then Canada. The United States beat Mexico and China by 5-0 scores. In the final at Chicago, Japan was defeated 5-0. Tilden played doubles in all three ties, teaming with Arnold Jones against Mexico, with Junior Coen against China and with George Lott against Japan. John Hennessey and Lott, along with Tilden, took care of the singles.

Tilden did not go to Paris for the French Championships but went to Wimbledon, where he lost to Rene Lacoste in the semi-final after beating Jean Borotra in the round of eight. Lacoste, who had lost to Henri Cochet in the French final, reversed the positions at Wimbledon by winning in four sets.

The Interzone final against Italy was to take place within the fortnight. On the eve of the draw Tilden was suspended by the USLTA because of articles he had written for an American newspaper commenting on the Wimbledon meeting. Samuel Collum, President of the USLTA and Joseph Wear, Chairman of the Davis Cup Committee, accompanied the American team and were aghast when the news was cabled to them. They had no choice but to withdraw Tilden from the match. However, with Frank Hunter and Hennessey playing the singles and Lott teaming with Hennessey in the doubles, only one match was lost.

The French were even more stupefied at the news. When they learned that they were to defend against only a youthful team they appealed to the Quai d'Orsay. The foreign office took the matter up with Myron Herrick, the American Ambassador. Herrick persuaded Collum to defy the Committee across the ocean. Collum reinstated Tilden. In the opening match he beat Lacoste. But Hennessey was no Bill Johnston. In the deciding match Cochet, on a court specially built for him, beat Tilden once more. On his return to America, Tilden was suspended until the end of the season. Cochet came to America and won the American title, beating Hunter in the final.

Before the 1929 French Championships commenced, a concrete stand was built around the Roland Garros center court, increasing the capacity to about 13,000. There were 23 challenges in the European Zone and 5 in the American. Australia did not compete and Monaco and Egypt were newcomers. Most of the teams still relied on older, more experienced players, but newcomers getting their first baptism of fire included Enrique Maier of Spain, George Lyttelton Rogers of Ireland, Louis Raymond and Norman Farquharson of South Africa, and H. W. "Bunny" Austin and G. P. "Pat" Hughes of Great Britain. In first round matches Czechoslovakia beat Austria, Belgium beat Roumania, Denmark beat Chile, Greece beat Yugoslavia, Hungary beat Norway, Monaco beat Switzerland and Egypt beat Finland. In the third round Germany beat Italy, Czechoslovakia beat Denmark, Hungary beat Holland and Great Britain beat South Africa. The finalists turned out to be Germany and Great Britain. The Germans became European Zone winners when they defeated Britain 3-2 at Berlin on July 12-14. The crucial match of this tie was when Prenn beat Austin 4-6, 6-2, 6-4, 4-6, 5-1, retired, the young Englishman being forced to default when a severe attack of cramps in his legs became unbearable. Austin attributed this to the weight and pressure of his perspiration-soaked flannel trousers and later adopted the expedient of having them cut off just below the knee. From this the vogue of men's shorts developed.

Tilden's suspension was lifted at the end of the year and, rather than waste his energies in the preliminary rounds of the American Zone, he went to Europe for the French and Wimbledon Championships. The three rounds in Montreal, Washington and Detroit were ably taken care of by John Hennessey and George Lott of the 1928 team, assisted by Wilmer Allison and John Van Ryn, who formed a doubles team for the first time in the final against Cuba.

Big Bill's experiences in Europe were none too happy. At Auteuil he lost to Lacoste in four sets in the semi-final. Borotra at last got the better of the nonchalant Cochet in the other half but lost to Lacoste in the final at 8-6 in the fifth set. At Wimbledon Tilden reached the semi-final but here he met Cochet, who won in three sets. Lacoste had an attack of bronchitis which kept him out of Wimbledon and the Davis Cup, too. Austin reached the Wimbledon semi-final—the first Englishman to do so since 1923—and lost to Borotra. Cochet turned the tables on Borotra and won his second All-England title. Each of the three Frenchmen now had two All-England Championships wins to his credit.

The Interzone final was played in Berlin. Tilden and Hunter in singles with Allison and Van Ryn in doubles, defeated Moldenhauer and Prenn

5-0. At Paris the following week, Lott played the second singles and lost to both Borotra and Cochet. Tilden beat Borotra but Cochet was never in trouble, the score being 6-3, 6-1, 6-2. Allison and Van Ryn won the second point for the United States with a straight set win over Borotra and Cochet.

None of the Frenchmen came to America that year, and Tilden won his seventh and last championship when he beat Hunter in the final.

The new Stade Roland Garros was completed in time for the 1930 Championships, and a beautiful creation it was. Around the outside of the enclosure were great boxes of flowers. There were ample dressing rooms for both sexes. A new scoreboard flashing lights for points, games and sets was installed and, at the ground floor level under the dressing rooms and boxes, there was a bar and restaurant. Twenty-four nations challenged in the European Zone, including Australia and Japan, leaving only Canada and Mexico to oppose the United States in the American Zone.

Harada, Ohta and Abe represented Japan and they came through to the final round, beating Hungary, India, Austria and Czechoslovakia on the way. Australia fielded Crawford, Hopman, Moon and Willard and reached the semi-final with wins over Switzerland, Ireland and Great Britain. Tloczynski was a new member of the Polish team, and H. G. N. Lee with Austin, Gregory and I. G. Collins represented Great Britain.

In the semi-final Italy defeated Australia at Milan 3-2 and beat Japan in the final at Genoa by the same score. Di Morpurgo, di Stefani and Gaslini were the European Champions from Italy.

Tilden again left the winning of the American Zone to Van Ryn, Lott, John Doeg and Allison. They joined Big Bill at Wimbledon after he had taken part in the French Championships. He set forth for the Riviera early in the winter, cleaned up everything in sight, got his timing adjusted to hard courts and arrived in Paris ready to take on all three Musketeers, if need be. Borotra's dashes for the net had no terrors for him. Lacoste had not shaken off his illness. Cochet remained. He was still the all-conquering magician who never bothered to train, who took no thought of the score and always believed in his own superiority. In the semi-final at Auteuil Tilden once more beat Borotra while Cochet was taking the measure of Morpurgo. The final was the same old story. Tilden won the first set but Cochet waved his wand and Big Bill was helpless.

Despite his assertion that play on grass never presented any more difficulty to him than play on hard courts, Cochet's experience at Wimbledon was not at all to his liking. Invincible at Paris, looking forward to another triumph over Tilden in the Davis Cup, he was feted and wined and dined. He kept putting off the unpleasant day when he must start to practice on grass. He waited too long. He met Wilmer Allison in the quarter-final and lost in straight sets. Tilden beat Borotra in one semi-final; Allison beat Doeg in the other. In the final Tilden beat his teammate in straight sets to win the All-England title for the third time, ten years after he had won his first.

Tilden did not play against Italy in the Interzone final at Roland Garros, but the youngsters took care of that. Allison lost to Morpurgo but Lott won both his matches and Allison-Van Ryn took the doubles. In the Challenge Round the following week, Tilden won the only match for United States when he again beat Borotra. Lott lost both his singles and Cochet-Brugnon defeated Allison-Van Ryn.

It was Tilden's swan song. In the American Championships he lost to John Doeg, who went on to win the title from Frank Shields. A few weeks later Tilden announced he had signed a moving picture contract which would make him a professional.

Three great figures had passed from the game in the last few years. First Johnston, then Lacoste, now Tilden. Henri the Nonchalant remained. He grew more careless, more confident, more magical in his recoveries as his old rivals passed over the horizon.

13

Hail Britannia

An important change took place in the draw for the 1931 contest. The former American Zone was divided into two parts – a North American and a South American Zone. Argentina beat Paraguay, Uruguay and Chile to win the South American title, while the United States had no trouble with Mexico and Canada. The Zone final was played at Washington on May 28, 29 and 30. Frank Shields and Sidney Wood, Nos. 2 and 4 in the 1930 ranking, played both singles and doubles for United States with Cliff Sutter, No. 5, substituting in the last singles. The result was a 5-0 win.

There were twenty-one challengers in the European Zone and several teams appeared with new faces. Among these were Fred Perry of Great Britain and Jiro Satoh of Japan. Perry was a husky, athletic youngster and an adept at table tennis. He soon found the outdoor game more to his liking and, with the encouragement of his father, a Labor member of Parliament, Perry was given the best of coaching and won the Argentine championship at Buenos Aires in 1930. Satoh had profited by the experience of his predecessors in opening with true Oriental patience. Then, when the moment came, he was all speed and fury.

The first two rounds were completed before the French Championships. Great Britain beat Monaco and Belgium without losing a set. Japan did the same to Yugoslavia. At Roland Garros disaster befell the British. Bunny Austin retired with a twisted ankle. Perry was beaten by Giorgio di Stefani. Henri Cochet did not compete. Jean Borotra beat Satoh in an exciting semi-final and won the title from his compatriot, Christian Boussus, after a seven-year interval.

England made a swift recovery with two more 5-0 wins over South Africa and Japan. Czechoslovakia, with Roderich Menzel and Ladislav Hecht carrying the load, beat Spain, Greece, Italy and Denmark to reach the final.

For the first time in eleven years the Americans had no Tilden to lead their crusade. George Lott and John Van Ryn were sent to Paris and won the French Doubles Championship. Frank Shields and Sidney Wood accompanied Gene Dixon, their Captain, to England. Neither was considered even an outside choice for the Wimbledon title.

Henri Cochet, despite his illness, was the favorite but again lost in the first round. Bunny Austin met Shields in one quarter-final and reached match point. He faltered and the American won. Fred Perry got one round farther without losing a set. Then Wood stopped him. Jean Borotra beat Satoh and faced Shields in the other semi-final. Leading two sets to one, Shields fell and twisted his ankle. He was given a twelve-minute massage. When the play was resumed, Borotra was no longer hot. It was another all-American final. Dixon refused to let Shields risk further injury. Wood won by default. Lott and Van Ryn beat Cochet and Brugnon in the doubles. It seemed as though nothing but an earthquake could stop the Americans from taking home the Cup.

After Great Britain beat the Czechs at Prague 4-1, they met the United States team in the Interzone final at Roland Garros on July 17-19. The Americans were ahead two rubbers to one at the end of the second day. Then Perry beat an erratic, over-confident Wood. Austin no longer hesitated to press home his victory against Shields. The following week France successfully defended the Cup when Cochet won both his singles and the doubles as well. Borotra lost to both Austin and Perry.

The British went home well-satisfied. They had reached the Challenge Round for the first time since 1919. The Americans had little to crow over, but they were not subdued for long. By the time they got home they were talking of winning next year. A new American star had been coming to the front in their absence.

In 1929 Ellsworth Vines and his friend, Keith Gledhill, won the Junior Doubles Championship. Gledhill was the better player at that time. Vines had greater ambition. He set about correcting his faults and announced that he was out to win the Championship and bring the Davis Cup back to America. His 1931 campaign was reminiscent of McLoughlin's invasion of 1912. He won at Seabright and Newport. He beat Shields and Perry in turn. In the Championships he came from behind to beat Perry again, and he won the title from Lott. In the spring of 1932 he was selected without question for the Davis Cup team.

Australia entered the North American Zone and drew a bye. Vines and Allison, with Van Ryn teaming with Allison in doubles, beat Mexico at New Orleans 5-0 and met Australia, winner over Cuba, at Philadelphia. Crawford and Hopman played all five matches for Australia. Vines, Shields, Allison and Van Ryn had no trouble winning another 5-0 victory. Brazil was the only challenger in the South American Zone and again the

Gottfried von Cramm of Germany. (Courtesy *World Tennis)*

North Americans whitewashed them and went across the Atlantic for the All-England tourney.

A new player was chosen with Prenn for the German team. He was Gottfried von Cramm, who was two months younger than Perry. He was of noble birth and was trained by Roman Najuch. In the 1931 French Championships he made a sorry showing against George Lott, but he came along swiftly in 1932. In the preliminary rounds of the Davis Cup the Germans defeated India, Austria and Ireland to reach the semi-final. The British reached the same round, with Lee and David alternating in singles along with Perry, while Perry and Hughes took care of the doubles. Italy and Japan were the other semi-finalists.

The Wimbledon entry list was one of the most representative since the war. Vines, Shields, Allison, Van Ryn and Wood were there, along with Cochet and Borotra of France, Satoh of Japan, and Austin and Perry of Great Britain. Cochet had just won his fifth French Championship. Again he was careless and took a nose dive to Ian Collins. In the final it was not Perry but Austin who stepped on the center court to meet Vines. The American had won his last two matches with the loss of only thirteen games. Austin won six. Vines was hailed as an unbeatable player who would handle Cochet just as roughly when they met at Roland Garros.

It was not the British who were the Americans' opponents in the Interzone final, but the Germans, who had beaten Perry, Austin and Hughes at Berlin. Austin lost both his matches and Perry the deciding one to Prenn. Italy was beaten at Milan 5-0. Shields and Vines were named for the singles and Allison and Van Ryn for the doubles. They had a close shave. Shields lost both his matches. Vines beat von Cramm with little to spare. Bernon Prentice, the American captain, decided to use Allison instead of Shields in the Challenge Round.

The French were having their troubles, too. Borotra was determined not to play again on hard courts. Lacoste entered the French Championships but found his old skill had left him. The Federation was desperate. It named Lacoste captain of the team, with the special mission of persuading Borotra to play. The Basque was unwilling, but in the end he put aside his preferences and yielded to the arguments of his comrade.

When Borotra gave himself, he gave without stint. He knew that all depended on the opening match. He stepped into everything Vines handed him. He dashed for the net with all his old furor. He fórced Vines into error after error and won in four sets. Cochet could do no less. Allison attacked courageously but the French had two points at the end of the first day. Even an American doubles victory did not lessen French confidence when Borotra faced Allison in the opening match on Sunday.

The Americans were in a desperate position. Even if Vines should beat Cochet in the last match, an Allison victory was essential. Allison had already spent himself by two days of hard play. Borotra had had a day's rest. Everything favored the Frenchman except the heavily watered court. Allison was cool and steady in the face of a bitterly hostile crowd. He won the first two sets. Borotra found himself in stroke as the court dried out. He pressed back the tiring American and won the third.

After the interval he came out refreshed and evened the score at two sets all. Now Allison rallied and reached 5-3. He had match point on Borotra's service. The Basque's second ball landed six inches beyond the service line. The players came forward to shake hands. The umpire called them back. The linesman had made no call. The score went back to deuce. Allison lost heart, while Borotra took advantage of his reprieve and won the match.

Nothing mattered now. America had suffered another humiliating defeat. Vines was discouraged. He took no interest in the outcome of the last match. Cochet won the first two sets with ridiculous ease. Prentice begged Vines to fight it out. The American came to life. Then the spectators saw the Vines of Wimbledon. Cochet was hammered into his first Davis Cup defeat since 1927. He sought his revenge in the American Championships. Vines improved on his Auteuil victory. The match lasted only fifty-nine minutes.

There had been lean years for Australia since 1920. Now they had a champion in Jack Crawford and a promising group of youngsters. The Australian Association invited an American team to visit them for a series of matches. Vines, Allison, Keith Gledhill and Van Ryn were sent. They did well at first. Before the Championship took place the heat and constant play finished them. Vines got only as far as the quarter-finals. The final was between Gledhill and Crawford, and the Australian won easily.

This year Australia challenged in the European Zone. They won their match against Norway and then went to Paris for the French Championships. Perry was beaten by Jiro Satoh. Crawford beat the Japanese in the semi-final and then conquered the fading Cochet. It was the first time a foreigner had won the French title.

When the European Zone ties were resumed in June, the four semi-finalists turned out to be Great Britain, Czechoslovakia, Australia and Japan. Great Britain reached this stage with wins over Spain, Finland and Italy. In their second match the Australians beat South Africa. The Czechs defeated Monaco and Greece and the Japanese were winners over Hungary, Ireland and Germany. England had now consolidated its team with Perry and Austin for the singles and Perry and Pat Hughes for the doubles. The Australians fielded Crawford and Vivian McGrath for singles and Crawford-Adrian Quist for the doubles. The British beat the Czechs 5-0, while Australia only squeaked through 3-2 against Japan.

At Wimbledon Perry lost in the first round to Norman Farquharson of South Africa. Satoh beat Bunny Austin. The semi-finalists were Vines, Cochet, Satoh and Crawford. For the second time within a month Crawford beat Satoh. For the third time within a year Vines proved he was Cochet's master. At the end of the eighth game of the fifth set of the final, Vines and Crawford were exactly even.

Now the effects of the Australian tour began to weight the scales. Vines was tired. Crawford was confident. He stood in to the American's vicious serves and won the deciding game at love.

The next week Australia and Great Britain met in the European Zone final. Perry was rested after his early defeat in the Championships. He saved the day by beating McGrath after Austin lost to Crawford. The British won the doubles and Austin's win from McGrath settled the issue. The British moved on to Paris.

The United States had an easy time winning the American Zone title from Mexico, Canada and Argentina. When this was settled, Allison, Lott, Van Ryn and Gledhill came directly to Paris without playing at Wimbledon. They were joined there by a weary and disheartened Vines. A sombre melancholy possessed him after his loss to Crawford. He was soon to be married. His income was next to nothing. His days from beginning to end of the year were filled with tennis. Tilden's agents were waving a professional contract under his nose. He was already a beaten man when he faced Austin in the opening match of the Interzone final. Allison had rested after his return from Australia. He was match shy. His doggedness was not worth even a set against Perry. Lott and Van Ryn won the doubles handily, but that was America's only point. Austin made sure of victory by beating Allison. Vines, fighting off the agony of a twisted ankle, collapsed on the court as Perry was about to drive home the winning thrust.

No persuasion could any longer induce Borotra to risk himself in singles. Lacoste chose in his place a young, aggressive player, Andre Merlin. Austin beat him in straight sets. Then Perry loosened the French hold on the Cup by beating Cochet in a match in which the Lyonnais was frequently booed by his victory-drunk compatriots. Roper Barrett was a shrewd captain. He sacrificed Lee and Hughes in the doubles to save Perry. The French added another point when Cochet beat Austin in a last ditch stand. Merlin rushed Perry off his feet to win the first set 6-4 and was within a point of taking the second. But Perry took himself in hand, pulled out the second set at 8-6 and won the next two 6-2, 7-5. Crowds, flashlights, reporters, banquets, gold watches and the congratulations of the King awaited the triumphant members of the British Davis Cup team on their arrival in London with the treasured Cup, which they last held just twenty years before.

14

Perry on Top of the World

Now that England was once again the Champion Nation, there remained only one more bridge to be crossed. The last Britisher who had won the Wimbledon title was Arthur Gore in 1909, the year Fred Perry was born. During that span of twenty-five years, four Australians, three Frenchmen and four Americans had won the coveted crown. It was time for an Englishman to show the world that an end had come to foreign domination.

Ellsworth Vines and Henri Cochet had become professionals. Jack Crawford had been beaten at Forest Hills. This was all that was needed to start Perry on the year-round trail. He was sure his stamina was equal to it. His father would not be satisfied until his son stood above them all. Perry crossed the American Continent and sailed for Australia. Crawford was still stale in January. Perry won the Australian Championship and he and Pat Hughes took the doubles.

The entries for 1934 competition for the Davis Cup reached such proportions that the Managing Committee scheduled a qualifying competition, which was held in the late summer of 1933. Seventeen European nations played three rounds. Italy, Switzerland, Austria and Germany qualified for the competition proper, which was held in the spring and early summer of 1934. India, France, Czechoslovakia, New Zealand and Japan joined the four qualifiers. Jean Borotra and Jacques Brugnon played only the doubles for France, the singles players being Christian Boussus and Andre Merlin. Jack Crawford and Vivian McGrath were the singles players for Australia, with Adrian Quist as Crawford's doubles partner. Roderich Menzel and Ladislav Hecht represented the Czechs. The Japanese had lost Jiro Satoh, who was ill and despondent and had taken his life by leaping into the sea from the ship which was carrying him and his teammates to Europe. Yamagishi, Fujikura and Nishimura composed the Japanese team.

When the French Championships commenced in May, Perry was the favorite. But he had never been fortunate at Paris. He twisted his ankle in his match with Giorgio di Stefani and the Italian beat him again (he won also in 1931). It was Gottfried von Cramm instead who faced Crawford in the final. The Australian was beaten by the splendid control and superior stamina of the young German.

In the Davis Cup quarter-finals, played from June 7 to 10, Czechoslovakia beat New Zealand 4-1; Italy beat Switzerland 5-0; France beat Germany 3-2, with von Cramm accounting for both Germany's wins; and Australia beat Japan 4-1, Fujikura's win over McGrath being the Nipponese's only point. The semi-finals were played the following week. The Czechs beat Italy at Milan 3-2, with di Stefani winning both his singles and Australia beat France at Paris, also 3-2. Andre Merlin was the star of this tie. He beat both Crawford and McGrath in four sets, the final between Czechoslovakia and Australia at Prague in July was another close one. Here it was Menzel, the tall, blond Czech, who won both his singles for his team's two points.

Only two ties were played in the North American Zone and the United States mades a clean seeep of both Canada and Mexico. Frank Shields, Sidney Wood, Les Stoefen, George Lott and John Van Ryn were the American players and were sent to England with Dick Williams as Captain.

By the time they got to Wimbledon, Crawford's confidence had returned. Perry, too, was in excellant form. They met in the final with Perry the winner. His countrymen cheered him to the echo. Wimbledon once more was British ground.

Britain now faced its first defense of the Davis Cup. Her old rivals, Australia and America, were the interzone finalists. Crawford had his glimpse of immortality when, with the score two rubbers to one for his team, he faced Sidney Wood on the third day. The American was in magnificent form and resolved to even the struggle. Crawford was helpless until rain caused postponement with Wood leading two sets to none. The next day Crawford got off to a good start and tied the score at two sets each, but it was beyond his powers to win three sets from so brillant an opponent. Shields' win from McGrath put the Americans in the Challenge Round.

It was a courageous uphill victory for the U. S., but the Americans were not able to repeat against the British. Perry was equal to the job, while Bunny Austin proved that Championship failures were no rehearsal for Davis Cup victories. The Americans won only the doubles. Perry closed a resplendent season by winning the American title from Allison for the second time.

The Melbourne Centenary was celebrated during the winter of

Frederick J. Perry of Great Britain. (Courtesy *World Tennis)*

1934-1935 with many sporting events. Perry was on hand to defend his title. He was not to escape, after all, the effects of year-round play. He suffered humiliating defeats in early matches. He improved during the Championships and won a straight-set victory over McGrath in the semi-final. But Crawford was at the top of his game and anxious for revenge. He beat Perry easily.

Again there was a qualifying round in the Davis Cup European Zone, played in the late summer of 1934 with 14 entries. The first round of the competition proper, played before the French Championships. left eight nations in the quarter-final–South Africa, Poland, Czechoslovakia, Japan, Australia, France, Germany and Italy.

Perry had been denied permission to sign a moving picture contract, which would have made him a professional. He arrived home in time to beat Austin in the final of the British Hard Court Championships. He crossed the Channel and won the French Championships for the first time, beating Crawford and von Cramm on successive days. When he beat these two again at Wimbledon, he made another record. He became the first champion since Tilden to hold the All-England title two years in a row.

A surprise winner of the European Zone turned up in Germany. Von Cramm had now reached technical maturity and, assisted by Henner Henkel and Denker, the Germans defeated Italy 4-1, Australia 4-1 and Czechoslovakia by the same score.

Four nations entered the North American Zone–The United States, China, Mexico and Canada. For America, these matches marked the beginning of the rise to stardom of a redheaded, freckle-faced Californian named John Donald Budge. Don didn't like tennis at first. He preferred baseball or basketball. When he won the first tournament he ever entered, he was on his way to the heights. In 1933 he got his first chance to play outside of California. He reached the final of the Clay Court Championships.

By 1935 Budge had made such progress that he was named to the Davis Cup team for the American Zone ties. With Bitsy Grant and Don's doubles partner, Gene Mako, no matches were lost and the team went to England for Wimbledon and the Interzone Final. In spite of his record, it was not expected that Budge would be selected to meet the Germans. But, like Tilden before him, his showing at Wimbledon, where he beat Austin in the quarter-final, gave him his chance. In the Interzones he met von Cramm for the first time and beat both him and Henkel in four sets. In the Challenge Round, with Wilmer Allison and John Van Ryn as his teammates, Budge was no match for either Perry or Austin. The British won all five matches.

Perry was now the unchallenged world's champion. He came to America to make it three in a row. In his match with Allison he fell and displaced a kidney. He put up only a brave but futile defense thereafter. In a one-sided final Wilmer Allison beat Sidney Wood for the first American victory since 1932.

In the first Championships of the 1936 season, Australia, Adrian Quist won the title from Jack Crawford. In the quarter finals he had beaten 18-year-old John Bromwich, the Junior Champion. "Brom," as his friends called him, had adopted the McGrath two-handed stroke and improved on it. He served with his right arm, took the forehand with his left, and played a two-fisted "backhand" from the right side.

Australia entered its team in the American Zone that year and, after the United States had beaten Mexico 5-0, met the Americans at Philadelphia over the Decoration Day week-end. Allison and Budge played the singles; Wilmer lost to Crawford and Quist, while Don won both of his. In the decisive doubles, Quist and Crawford beat Budge and Mako 4-6, 2-6, 6-4, 7-5, 6-4.

In the European Zone the preliminary competition had been abandoned and seventeen nations completed two rounds before the French Championships began. Austria, Belgium, Yugoslavia, France, Germany, Argentina, Ireland and Switzerland qualified for the quarter-final.

Perry beat Austin to win his fifth British Hard Court Championship, but misfortune again crossed his path at Paris. This time it was von Cramm who defeated him in the final by the peculiar score of 6-0, 2-6, 6-2, 2-6, 6-0.

It was a foregone conclusion that Germany would be the European Zone winners, but they were faced in the final by the greatly strengthened Yugoslav team of Franjo Puncec, Drago Mitic, Josip Pallada and Franjo Kukuljevic. They had earlier defeated France and Australia. Only three matches were played at Zagreb in the final. Henkel and von Cramm won both singles and only the doubles was close.

The Interzone final was played at Wimbledon on July 18-21. Gottfried von Cramm's win over Quist at 11-9 in the fifth set was Germany's only victory. The Challenge Round, played the following week, resulted in a narrow 3-2 win for the defending British team. Both Perry and Austin beat Crawford, but Austin lost to Quist and, in the doubles, Hughes and Tuckey lost to Crawford and Quist 6-4, 2-6, 7-5, 10-8.

Perry returned to the United States and recaptured his American title in a final against Budge, marked by the Englishman's apparent nonchalance and by Budge's failure to take advantage of his opportunities. At the end of the season, after losing to Budge at Los Angeles, Perry became a

Left: Wilmer L. Allison, U. S. champion 1935, being congratulated by Frederick J. Perry of Great Britain. (Courtesy *World Tennis)*

professional and signed to meet Vines in a series of matches during the winter. The British renaissance was over.

15

On the Move

With Fred Perry's exit from the amateur ranks it was certain that, barring a miracle, England could not hold the Cup. So interest centered on the three leading contenders – America, Australia and Germany.

Australia again challenged in the American Zone, along with the United States, Japan and Mexico. With Don Budge and Frank Parker playing the singles and Budge and Gene Mako the doubles, the United States defeated Japan at San Francisco on April 30-May 2. Yamagishi won the only set for Nippon against Parker.

Australia met Mexico in Mexico City and also won 5-0. Adrian Quist and Vivian McGrath played the singles for Australia with young John Bromwich winning the final singles. Esteban Reyes and Ricardo Tapia were the Mexican singles players, while Unda and Hernandez lost to Crawford and Quist in the doubles.

The final between Australia and the United States was played at Forest Hills over the Decoration Day holiday and was another walkover. Quist was indisposed. Crawford and Bromwich were the singles players for Australia while Budge and Bitsy Grant represented United States. Bromwich took the only set when he met Budge. Budge-Mako beat Crawford-McGrath 7-5, 6-1, 8-6.

Twenty nations entered the European Zone and two rounds were completed by May 17 with Germany, Italy, Belgium, Sweden, Yugoslavia, South Africa, Czechoslovakia and France qualifying for the quarter-finals.

Gottfried von Cramm of Germany was not permitted to enter the singles in the French Championships on the theory that Henner Henkel, a fellow countryman, might well win and thus gain confidence and stature. So it turned out. Henkel beat Bunny Austin in the final and the German pair won the doubles.

Two more rounds in the Davis Cup were played before Wimbledon. Germany beat Italy at Milan 4-1; Belgium beat Sweden at Brussels 3-2; Yugoslavia beat South Africa at Zagreb 4-1; and Czechoslovakia beat

France at Prague by the same score. The two-man teams of Germany with von Cramm and Henkel and Czechoslovakia with Roderich Menzel and Ladislav Hecht proved themselves the class of Europe by beating Belgium and Yugoslavia repectively to enter the final round.

Wimbledon was almost completely an American triumph. Budge had no difficulty in his half and lost his only set to Frankie Parker in the semi-final. In the other half von Cramm had stouter opposition. The score of the final between Budge and von Cramm was 6-3, 6-4, 6-2 for the American. Budge and Mako won the doubles from Pat Hughes and Tuckey.

The Germans returned to Berlin for the European Zone final against the Czechs. Von Cramm had a tough match with Menzel amid boos from the partisan crowd at Menzel's stalling tactics. After losing the first two sets to the tall, blond Czech, von Cramm took the next three 6-4, 6-3, 6-2. Henkel took Hecht's measure in straight sets and clinched their victory with a four-set win of the doubles. In the final match between substitutes, Cejnar beat Denker to give the Czechs their only point.

Meanwhile, in London, the American team, under Captain Walter Pate, tuned up their strokes for the coming encounter. There was no question that Budge would be the No. 1 singles player nor that Budge and Mako would play the doubles. The choice of the second singles player lay between Parker and Bitsy Grant. There was considerable surprise when Pate selected Grant to play against the Germans. Bitsy had done nothing at Wimbledon, while Frank had reached the semi-final and had won the only set from Budge. But Pate felt that if anyone other than Budge could win a match, Grant had just the type of game which was likely to beat Henkel. As it turned out, it was the insistence of the German Captain, Kleinschroth, that Henkel constantly come to the net that upset Pate's plan. Both the Germans beat Grant, Budge beat Henkel and the Americans won the doubles. The issue hung on the last match between Budge and von Cramm.

This was not only one of the finest exhibitions of tennis ever played but one of the most thrilling matches. Von Cramm was in superb form. He won the first two sets and, after Budge had taken the third and fourth, held a 4-1 lead in the fifth. But Budge never lost his courage nor aplomb. As he crossed over he whispered to Pate, "Don't worry, Cap. I'll make it." He continued to carry the fight to von Cramm. In the fourteenth game of the final set and on the sixth match point, victory came to him.

The Challenge Round against the British the following week-end was an anticlimax. Parker was chosen by Pate for the singles and lost to Bunny Austin in straight sets. Charles Hare was drawn against Budge and carried him to a 15-13 first set but was helpless thereafter. Budge and Mako beat Tuckey and Wilde in the doubles in four long sets, and Parker won the decisive point on the third day when he beat Hare 6-2, 6-4, 6-2.

The Germans accompanied the victorious American team on their way home and an English team headed by Hare followed. In the doubles at Longwood, von Cramm and Henkel avenged their defeat by a straight set win from Budge-Mako. At Forest Hills Hare took the first two sets from von Cramm in one semi-final. Parker lost to Budge in the other. Though the German carried the final to five sets, there was never any doubt of Budge's superiority. The thrills of the Davis Cup meeting were not repeated.

The rivals met again with the same result in the final of the Pacific Southwest tournament. Soon thereafter the Germans, with Budge and Mako, set off for Australia. In an exhibition match, best of three sets, von Cramm scored his only win over Budge.

In the early days of 1938, Budge beat John Bromwich in the final of the Australian Championships, the first American since Fred Alexander in 1908 to carry off the honors. Those who looked forward to another Budge-von Cramm thriller were disappointed. Bromwich had put out the German in the semi-final.

The Americans had scarcely reached home when the entire tennis world was shocked by the news that von Cramm had been arrested on his arrival in Germany. The Nazis tried to keep the affair secret, but inquiries through the Dutch legation in Berlin brought to light the fact that von Cramm was charged with a moral offense. Many of his friends in other countries refused to believe this, and it was rumored that Henkel had informed against him. Whatever the truth might have been, von Cramm was lost to the German team.

Nevertheless, the Germans found a worthy substitute in an Austrian, Georg von Metaxa, and with Henkel leading the way they entered, with 16 other nations, in the European Zone. The other teams were mostly a mixture of old and yet untried players. France, with Bernard Destremau and a newcomer, Yvon Petra, reached the quarter-final, while Great Britain, with Butler, Shayes and Wilde, did not survive its second match. The most improved team was that of Yugoslavia, which first defeated Czechoslovakia and then Great Britain. The Yugoslav players were Franjo Puncec, Drago Mitic, Josip Pallada and Franjo Kukuljevic.

The quarter-final matches were played the last week of May and were followed by the French Championships and Wimbledon. Budge won both titles, and with no von Cramm or Perry to oppose him found the going easier than before.

Don Budge and Gene Mako brought the Cup back to America in 1937. (Courtesy *World Tennis)*

The Davis Cup European Zone semi-finals, played from July 21 to 23, found Germany the winner over France at Berlin by 3 rubbers to 2 and Yugoslavia the victor over Belgium at Brussels by 5-0. At Berlin on July 29-31, Germany became the European Zone winner for the fourth time.

Only Japan, Mexico and Canada challenged Australia in the American Zone. Yamagishi and Nakano beat Canada at Montreal 5-0, and at Kansas City Bromwich and Quist beat Mexico by the same score. The final between Australia and Japan was played at Montreal on August 12-14. John Bromwich lost both his singles, giving Australia a narrow 3-2 victory. The Interzone final between Germany and Australia was played the following week at Longwood and the Australians did not lose a set.

For the Challenge Round at Germantown over the Labor Day week-end, Captain Pate called on Budge and Bobby Riggs for the singles and Budge-Mako for the doubles. Riggs was a young Californian who was Junior Champion in 1935 and had been ranked just behind Budge at No. 2 in 1937, ahead of Parker and Grant. He was a fine all-court player, relying on uncanny anticipation and skillful tactics. Budge won both his singles and Riggs beat Adrian Quist in four sets, giving the defending champions a 3-2 victory.

The Singles Championships at Forest Hills were marked by a series of upsets. Gilbert Hunt beat Riggs. Bromwich, after winning from Parker and Joe Hunt, lost in the semi-final to Mako. The final between the two doubles partners was comparatively easy for Budge. With this win Don completed his Grand Slam, the first player ever to win the four major titles in the same year.

On November 10, in Walter Pate's office, Budge signed a contract to play as a professional. If it was the right moment for him to capitalize on his fame, it was also evident that his removal from the amateur ranks would leave a void difficult to fill when the Davis Cup was again the objective of an Australian challenge.

In the fall of 1938 Czechoslovakia had been surrendered to Germany and the Czech No. 1 player, Roderich Menzel, became a German. Von Metaxa, an Austrian, had taken German citizenship the previous year. While this accession added strength to the German team and enabled it to reach the European Zone final, it was the fast-coming Yugoslavs who carried off the honors. Twenty nations entered the 1939 contest, with Belgium, Yugoslavia, Germany and Great Britain reaching the semi-finals. The Yugoslavs beat the Belgians at Zagreb, by 3 rubbers to 2, and Germany beat the British team of Hare, Shayes, Wilde and Shaffi 5-0. In the final at Zagreb, the Yugoslavs broke the Germans' string with a 3-2 win and qualified to come to America as the European Representatives for the first time.

Australia had an easy road in the American Zone, beating Mexico, the Philippines and Cuba in turn without the loss of a set. In the Interzone final Bromwich unaccountably lost the opening rubber to Puncec but that was all.

Meanwhile Riggs and his doubles partner, Elwood Cooke, were sent to Paris for the French Championships. Also there was Don McNeill, who had made a winter tour of India, China and Japan. This entensive play on hard courts put McNeill in fine form for Roland Garros. He not only beat Riggs in the final but won the doubles also with Charles Harris. Wimbledon, however, was a different story. Riggs and Cooke met in the final, with Riggs the winner. Together they won the doubles. Riggs also won the mixed with Alice Marble.

The Merion Cricket Club was the scene of the Davis Cup Challenge Round, with Riggs and Parker nominated for the singles. A third member of the team was Joe Hunt, now a midshipman at Annapolis, who was expected to play the doubles with Riggs. As a reserve, Captain Pate chose young Jack Kramer, the 1936 Boys' Champion and the 1939 Junior Doubles Champion. At the end of the first day the Americans were two up with three to go. As it seemed almost certain that Riggs would win the third point when he met Quist, Pate decided to gamble on the doubles and named Hunt and Kramer as the American pair. Though they enthused the spectators by winning the first set and carrying the third to 7-5, the youngsters never really had a chance against such a seasoned pair as Quist and Bromwich. Riggs made a good fight against Quist, pulling up to two sets all after losing the first two. In the fifth he was done and Australia had tied the score. When Parker lost to Bromwich 6-0, 6-3, 6-1, Australia had recaptured the Cup.

The Second World War had now commenced with Germany's invasion of Poland. As in 1914, the Australians had no desire to enter the American Championships. In the semi-finals Bromwich was beaten by Welby Van Horn, a newcomer from California whose battering-ram style had caught the fancy of the spectators. He was the crowd's favorite when he met Riggs in the final. But he had run out his string and Riggs won the title in straight sets. The Australians were not disheartened. They had got what they came for. They left the Cup in safekeeping in New York until the end of the war and departed joyously for home, the Champion Nation for the seventh time.

16

The "Big Game"

When the Second World War commenced in September, 1939, it was evident that, as in World War I, tennis would suffer an eclipse. Before many months had elapsed, the entire continent of Europe and Great Britain were involved in the conflict. When the Japanese bombed Pearl Harbor in December, 1941, the holocaust became world-wide.

The Italian, French and Wimbledon Championships were suspended for the duration. Australia was far removed from the battle lines until the flames spread to the Pacific, so the Championships were held as usual in January, 1940. Quist won the singles and teamed with Bromwich to take the doubles.

Among the early casualties in Europe was Henner Henkel, von Cramm's partner on the German Davis Cup team of 1937. Tony Mottram, the leading British player, was an R. A. F. officer. Bernard Destremau, the rising Frenchman, joined the resistance after the fall of France. The Germans and the Vichy government took charge, the National Championships were resumed in France. Only in America did tennis players go about their business as if the war was no concern of theirs. Lacking international competition, few new players of world class came to the fore.

Bobby Riggs, the 1939 American and Wimbledon Champion, played the grass court circuit and met another Californian, Frank Kovacs, in the Seabright final, winning in the fifth set. At Forest Hills he lost to Don McNeill after winning the first two sets. Frank Parker, Jack Kramer, Ted Schroeder and Joe Hunt, all Boys' or Junior Champions, along with Billy Talbert of Cincinnati and Gardnar Mulloy of Florida, were the leaders in the 1940 ranking, behind McNeill, Riggs and Kovacs. Kramer beat Schroeder were the Doubles Champions.

In the Championships, Riggs took charge again. Kovacs beat McNeill in one semi-final while Riggs beat Schroeder in the other. Kovacs took the first set of the final at 7-5 but Riggs won the next three. Kramer and Schroeder repeated their win of the doubles.

During the winter Riggs and Kovacs became professionals. McNeill got a commission in the Navy. Soon most of the other top-ranking players were in the service. Joe Hunt was a midshipman at Annapolis. Frank Parker was an Army Sergeant. Jack Kramer enlisted in the Coast Guard. Ted Schroeder was in the Navy. Gar Mulloy commanded an LST. Still, as tournament time approached, most of these players were able to get sufficient leave from their commands to enter the Nationals.

Among the newcomers in 1942 was a short, swarthy, pigeon-toed visitor from Ecuador, Francisco Segura. The National Doubles was won for the first time by Mulloy and Talbert. At Forest Hills Schroeder and Parker came through to the final, with Schroeder the winner. With Ted at the top of the ranking, Parker, Mulloy, Segura and Talbert followed.

With the growing involvement of the United States in the War, there was some question whether the 1943 Championships would be held. It was eventually decided to go ahead on a limited basis with all five National Championships played at Forest Hills. Entries were held to thirty-two singles and sixteen teams in singles and sixteen teams in doubles, with the first two rounds best of three sets. Segura, Kramer, Hunt and Talbert reached the semi-final. Kramer beat Segura in one half. Hunt beat Talbert in the other. The final went to four sets with Hunt the winner. Kramer and Parker won the doubles.

Shortly after his victory, Joe Hunt, one of the most likeable and promising players of his time, was killed in an airplane training maneuver. Hunt's absence in 1944 brought his first Championship to Frank Parker, although he had been ranked in the Top Ten since 1933. Yet, coming up to the Nationals, Parker had won no outstanding tournament. Talbert and Segura were the favorites at Forest Hills. With McNeill and Parker they reached the semi-finals. Parker and Talbert met in the final. The singles title he had long coveted once more eluded Talbert when Parker's superior stamina overcame Bill's flawless stroking.

With the War at an end in the summer of 1945, preparations were made to resume the Championships on a scale approaching their pre-war scope. In addition to Parker, Talbert and Segura, who were seeded in that order, the field included a sizeable contingent of South American and Canadian players. In winning his match with Segura, Talbert pulled a muscle in his leg which handicapped him severely in the final against Parker. He struggled bravely through a 14-12 first set but was helpless thereafter. Mulloy joined Talbert to win back the doubles title.

With peace restored, all international championships were resumed in 1946. Bromwich and Quist returned to action to win the Australian singles and doubles. A new Aussie player, Dinny Pails, was a close contender.

Fifteen nations entered the Davis Cup European Zone and the semi-finalists turned out to be Yugoslavia, France, Sweden and Belgium. Great Britain, with a patched up team, lost in the first round to France which fielded four prewar players – Yvon Petra, Pierre Pellizza, Marcel Bernard, and Bernard Destremau. Yugoslavia also relied on its pre-war team, while Jaroslav Drobny appeared for the first time for Czechoslovakia. Other newcomers were Philippe Washer for Belgium and Lennart Bergelin and Torsten Johansson for Sweden.

A new Pacific Section of the American Zone was constituted, with New Zealand the only entry. In the North American Section, Mexico beat Canada and the United States beat the Philippines, both by 5-0 scores. The United States won the final and New Zealand defaulted to give the U. S. a walkover. Parker, Talbert and Mulloy were the American team.

The Wimbledon Championships preceded the French that year. There was a full entry of 128, including the Australians Dinny Pails, Geoff Brown and Harry Hopman. Kramer and Tom Brown, a young San Franciscan, represented America and teamed to win the doubles, although they had never played together before. Pails and Kramer were the top seeds. Kramer, suffering from a badly blistered hand, met Drobny in the fourth round. Although he carried the match to five close sets, the Czech was the winner. Petra beat Pails in the quarters and Tom Brown in the semi-final after losing the first two sets. Geoff Brown beat Drobny in three. The final was a terrific struggle, with Petra finally coming through.

At Roland Garros Petra gave a poor display and was beaten by his teammate, Marcel Bernard, in the semi-final. In the other semi-final, Drobny beat Tom Brown in the fifth set. Bernard won the title after losing the first two sets to the Czech.

In the Davis Cup semi-finals, Yugoslavia beat France at Paris 3-2, while Sweden had a 4-1 victory over Belgium. The final, played at Varberg, Sweden, with Franjo Puncec on the sideline from illness, resulted in a Swedish win by three rubbers to two.

Thirty-three foreign players entered the American Championships, including the Wimbledon Champion, Washer from Belgium and Hopman from Australia. None of the foreigners reached the quarter-finals. Kramer dropped but one set to McNeill. Bob Falkenburg was taken to the fifth set by Talbert. Mulloy beat Segura. The surprise of the round was Tom Brown's win from Parker. He continued his sensational play against Mulloy and, before a crowded and enthusiastic house, led Kramer in the first set of the final. Kramer then increased the pressure, won the set at 9-7 and had no difficulty thereafter. Mulloy and Talbert won their third doubles title.

Bergelin and Johansson came to America for the Interzone tie and met the United States team at Forest Hills. Kramer and Parker won all four singles; Mulloy and Talbert took the doubles.

These four were obvious choices for the team to go to Australia for the Challenge Round. Walter Pate was again the Captain. Two other players were added as insurance—Tom Brown, finalist at Forest Hills, and Ted Schroeder. Schroeder, now a business man and week-end player, had not come East for the Nationals nor had he played in any of the American Zone ties. But he was Kramer's doubles partner and had carried Jack to four sets in the Pacific Southwest tournament.

A week after arriving in Melbourne, Tom Brown fell ill with influenza and asked to withdraw from the team. Talbert felt he was not playing his best. The four selected by Pate, with the approval of all the players, were Kramer, Schroeder, Mulloy and Parker. Mulloy felt strongly that he should have been chosen for the doubles as he and Parker had consistently beaten Kramer and Schroeder in practice. Parker claimed that he had been promised one of the singles posts. He was furious when Schroeder was chosen in his place and refused to play at all. So Pate named the two Californians for both singles and doubles.

The Australian selectors also had their troubles. John Bromwich and Dinny Pails were automatically chosen as the singles players. Geoff Brown was dropped, and Adrain Quist and Colin Long were among those considered as a partner for Bromwich in the doubles. Quist was eventually chosen.

The critics were unanimous in their opinion that Australia would win, either by 4-1 or 3-2, on the assumption that "Brom" could not lose and that Quist and Bromwich would regain their pre-war form to take the doubles. The end result was the worst defeat ever inflicted on a holding champion since the competition began, the total score for the United States being 5 rubbers, 15 sets and 101 games to 2 sets and 68 games.

The temperature was over 100 when Schroeder took the court against Bromwich in the first match. Ted was a different man from the one Brom had beaten in straight sets in the Victorian Championships, a few days earlier. He got off the mark quickly and forced the play. The first set was won by Australia but after that, except for a letdown in the fourth which Bromwich won at love, Schroeder was on top throughout. The crowd waited for Bromwich to reveal his form but in vain. The first rubber went to the United States 3-6, 6-1, 6-2, 0-6, 6-3.

The second match between Pails and Kramer was a fine exhibition of free, hard play. Kramer was a little off his game at the start, but once he got into his stride he was in command throughout the match. The better

John Bromwich (left) and Ted Schroeder (U.S.) toss before their match in 1946. (Courtesy *World Tennis)*

Pails played, the more Kramer increased the pace. The score for Kramer was 8-6, 6-2, 9-7.

In the doubles, most of the interest on the side of the Australians was how Quist would play. It was felt a risk had been taken in naming him, but he played as well as the Americans allowed him and there was little between him and Bromwich. Kramer and Schroeder took the first four games with the loss of only 7 points. Their net rushing tactics could not be countered by the Australian team, and overhead they dealt mercilessly with anything tossed up to them. Australia managed to save two games in this set and, when they took the score to 4-1 in the second, the hopes of the crowd soared. From 5-4 to Bromwich, Kramer and Schroeder lost only four more points to take the set at 7-5. With the score 4-2 for the United States in the third set Australia's final effort came when Quist served to make it 3-4. He and Bromwich then won Schroeder's service for 4-all. Bromwich lost the first two points on his service but evened at 30-all. Two more points for Kramer and the chance for a lead disappeared. Kramer, serving beautifully, made no mistakes and Schroeder finished the match by smashing the ball down the sideline out of Brom's reach.

Rain interrupted play on the next day and, when the tie was resumed on Monday, Kramer settled the question of who would be ranked No. 1 in the world for 1946 by beating Bromwich convincingly 8-6, 6-4, 6-4. Mulloy substituted for Schroeder in the final match and here, too, the result was seldom if ever in doubt. Mulloy seemed able to make any pace that suited him and the score of 6-3, 6-3, 6-4 tells its own story.

This victory did more than bring about a change in the holders. It established the supremacy of the "big game." In essence, it emphasized an attacking pattern of play rather than the more defensive strategy based on sound ground strokes. Neither Bromwich nor Quist nor Pails was an attacking player. When Pate selected Schroeder and Kramer as his team, he recognized that the serve and volley game was the surest way to victory.

17

Australia Learns a Lesson

Twenty nations challenged for the Davis Cup in the European Zone in 1947 but only two, Australia and Canada, challenged in the American Zone. In the third round in the European Zone, South Africa beat Great Britain and Yugoslavia beat Belgium, each by four matches to one, while Czechoslovakia beat New Zealand and France beat Monaco five matches to none.

At Wimbledon Jack Kramer swept everything before him. Tom Brown was his opponent in the final and Kramer-Bob Falkenburg won the doubles.

In the Davis Cup semi-finals, Yugoslavia beat South Africa three matches to two and Czechoslovakia beat France four matches to one. In the final round played at Zagreb, Czechoslovakia became the European Zone winner by four matches to love.

In the American Zone Australia beat Canada at Montreal by five matches to none. The interzone final was also played at Montreal and Drobny won the only match for the Czechs when he beat Pails in four sets.

The Challenge Round was played at Forest Hills before the American Championships. Kramer and Ted Schroeder were the American team, John Bromwich and Dinny Pails again played the singles for Australia while Colin Long replaced Adrain Quist in the doubles. The result was a four to one victory for the United States, the Australians winning only the doubles.

In the American Championships, Kramer and Schroeder won the National Doubles for the third time. At Forest Hills Kramer had no trouble until the final. There he met Frank Parker, who had beaten Bromwich. As usual, the spectators favored the underdog. Parker rewarded them by carrying the fight to five sets. Kramer then went on to win both the Pacific Southwest and Pacific Coast titles.

With Kramer a professional in 1948, Parker, Schroeder, Gar Mulloy and Billy Talbert, next in the ranking, were expected to fight it out for the top honors. But it remained for another of the "big game" exponents, Richard (Pancho) Gonzales, then not even ranked in the First Ten, to come to the top like a bombshell.

A boy of Mexican parentage, Gonzales taught himself the game on the cement courts of Southern California. Eventually he came to the notice of Perry Jones, the mastermind of California tennis. But Pancho was not interested in schooling nor in the social amenities Jones insisted on. All he wanted to do was to play tennis. So Jones abandoned the boy to his own devices until the year he became 19. He was sent East in 1948 and by the end of the season his name was on everyone's tongue.

The French Federation sent Jean Borotra and Marcel Bernard to the American Indoors and they won the doubles. Parker went to Paris and won the French Championships. At Wimbledon it was another American, Bob Falkenburg, who came through to beat Bromwich and continue the American reign. The Australians proved their mastery of the doubles game when Bromwich and his young compatriot, Frank Sedgman, won the doubles from Tom Brown and Mulloy.

There were 25 entries in the European Zone for the Davis Cup but only four in the American Zone. In the European semi-finals, Lennart Bergelin and Torsten Johansson of Sweden beat the British team of Tony Mottram and Geoff Paish by four matches to one while the Czechs–Jaroslav Drobny and Vladimir Cernik–beat Gianni Cucelli and Marcello Del Bello of Italy three matches to two. In the final, played at Prague after Wimbledon, the Czechs became European Zone Champions by four matches to one.

In America, Mexico beat Canada at Montreal 4-1 while Australia beat Cuba at Havana 3-0. The final was played at Mexico City. Quist lost to Gustavo Palafox but the Australians won all the other rubbers. The Interzone final was held at Longwood and the Australians had a narrow escape. Leading 2-1 on the third day, Quist lost the opening rubber to Drobny by scores of 6-8, 3-6, 18-16, 6-3, 7-5, but Cernik was no match for Billy Sidwell. At Forest Hills it was once more no contest. Parker won both his matches in straight sets while Schroeder dropped one set to Quist. Talbert and Mulloy, the American champions, beat Sidwell and Colin Long 8-6 9-7, 2-6, 7-5.

Gonzales commenced his trek to the East by winning the Western and Clay Court titles. But he was unaccustomed to grass and did little in the tune-up tournaments which preceded Forest Hills. He was not even considered for the Davis Cup Team. In the Nationals he was so little regarded that he was the last of the eight American seeds. He first proved his class when he beat Parker in the quarter-final. Drobny, Herb Flam, and the smooth-stroking South African, Eric Sturgess, were the other semi-finalists. Pancho had a tough battle against Drobny. Sturgess had no trouble with Flam.

A long women's final delayed the start of the men's title match to a late hour. Gonzales started at such a devastating pace in the first two sets that Sturgess seemed to be outclassed. In the third set Sturgess' fine ground strokes held the American in check for twenty-four games. By that time it was almost dark and the referee notified the players that only three more games could be played. Luckily Gonzales needed only two to win the Championship. Returning with his laurels to the Pacific Coast, he was not so happy. Ted Schroeder had always been his nemesis and proved he was the better man again.

Early in 1949 Gonzales had the satisfaction of beating Schroeder at La Jolla but Ted got his revenge in May. Gonzales and Parker entered the French Championships and were seeded one and two. Budge Patty beat Pancho in the semi-final and Parker won the title. The two Americans easily won the doubles.

Schroeder, who had never before played at Wimbledon, joined Parker, Gonzales, Patty, Falkenburg and Mulloy at the All-England Club. The Australian contingent included Bromwich and Geoff Brown as well as the new Australian Champion, Sedgman. Gonzales started off with three easy matches and then lost to Geoff Brown. All the quarter-final matches went to five sets. Schroeder lost the first two to Sedgman but won in a 9-7 fifth set. He had to come from behind again to beat Sturgess. The final was Ted's third five-setter in a row, but he beat Drobny in the end.

There were twenty-two entries in the Davis Cup European Zone that year and four in the American. In Europe the semi-finalists were France, Hungary, Italy and Yugoslavia. Sweden was beaten by the Yugoslavs and the Czechs lost to France in the third round. In the final, played after Wimbledon, Cucelli and Del Bello beat Robert Abdesselam and Marcel Bernard of France 3 matches to 2. Australia and Mexico were the finalists in the American Zone, and Sedgman and Bromwich did not lose a match. They had no trouble when they met Italy at Rye. At Forest Hills it was Schroeder and Gonzales against Sidwell and Sedgman. The only rubber lost by the Americans was when Sidwell and Bromwich beat Talbert and Mulloy. Though young Sedgman had lost both his matches, he gave indications that the Australians would soon cease to be doormats.

In the American Championships Gonzales and Schroeder were seeded one and two. Schroeder had to go to five sets to beat Sedgman and Talbert to reach the final. Pancho had a somewhat easier road through Art Larsen and Frank Parker. The final between the defending champion and the Wimbledon winner was one of the most exciting ever played at Forest Hills. The first set went to 34 games, with Schroeder the winner. Ted followed with a 6-2 win of the second set. It seemed as if the nemesis was still potent and that Pancho was through. But he took the third at 6-1 when Ted momentarily faltered. After the intermission it was all Pancho. At the end of the season Gonzales and Parker became professionals.

The despondency in Australia following four successive defeats in the Challenge Round, together with the hopes aroused by the Americans' loss of Kramer, Parker and Gonzales to the professionals, led the Australian Association to seek new leadership. Harry Hopman was named captain of the Down Under team for 1950.

Hopman was forty-four years old and primarily a doubles player in his prime, His most notable singles win was over Don Budge in the final of the Pacific Coast tournament in 1938. He had captained the victorious Australian team in 1939 but had not been considered for the job since the war.

Hopman was a keen strategist and a most successful developer of young players. Above all, he was a disciplinarian and insisted on a rigorous training program for his men, including gymnasium work and running. He had been largely responsible for the progress Frank Sedgman had made. He realized, better than anyone else, that unless the fading stars of the pre-war era were replaced by young men who had learned the big game of the Americans, more setbacks could be expected. He set about to find another player like Sedgman for his team. His eye fell on Ken McGregor, a soccer football star who also had a liking for tennis. Hopman trained McGregor in the serve and volley game. He believed that success in the coming Davis Cup encounter would not only consolidate his own position and prove his theories of training and play, but would also stimulate even younger players, still in their teens, to follow his precepts.

In America no one had Hopman's foresight. Gonzales and Parker were gone. Schroeder played only in California, Talbert and Mulloy were still the leading doubles team. Below them in the First Ten were a group of players, none of whom was considered to be a Davis Cup prospect. Vic Seixas, No. 12, Dick Savitt, No. 16, and Tony Trabert, No. 23, were not yet ready.

In the early season Budge Patty won the French Championships with a five-set victory over Jaroslav Drobny. Talbert and his young protege, Tony Trabert, won the doubles. At Wimbledon the Australians appeared in force. Bromwich and Quist took the doubles. Sedgman came through to the singles final, where he lost to an inspired Patty in four sets.

In America, Larsen, Flam, Schroeder, Savitt, and Seixas won and lost, with none of them showing any marked superiority. Who, but who, would be named to the defending Davis Cup team? Patty, the French and Wimbledon titleholder, was an obvious choice. He and Schroeder were paired for the National Doubles and Patty was seeded No. 1 in the Singles Championships. But an ankle injury which befell him at Newport caused his withdrawal from both events.

Twenty-two nations, including two from Asia—the Philippines and Pakistan—challenged in the European Zone in 1950. Kurt Nielson and Torben Ulrich of Denmark had come to the fore and won a surprise victory in the semi-finals against the veteran Italian team of Cucelli and the del Bello brothers by 4 rubbers to 1. Sven Davidson joined Lennart Bergelin and Torsten Johansson for Sweden and beat Poland by five rubbers to love. Sweden beat Denmark in the European Zone final and sent their team to America, where they met the Australians in the Interzone final at Rye. Bergelin was the sensation of the tie. He beat both Sedgman and Bromwich. The doubles win of the Australians was the deciding point.

When the two captains, Hopman and Alrick Man, met at Forest Hills to name their teams for the Challenge Round, it was learned that McGregor, instead of Bromwich, would play the second singles for Australia. Though McGregor had played in the Mexican tie as a substitute when the result had already been decided, Hopman had craftily withheld him at Rye and his naming now was a complete surprise. For the United States, the only surprise was that the team contained no new faces. Ted Schroeder, twenty-nine, Tom Brown, twenty-eight, Gar Mulloy, thirty-six, and Bill Talbert, thirty-two were chosen. At the end of the second day the Australians had already won the Cup. Sedgman ran through Brown in straight sets. McGregor did the same to Schroeder. The doubles went to five sets. On the final day Sedgman beat Schroeder to bring the score to 4-0. In the last match Tom Brown called on all his old wizardry to beat McGregor.

18

The Whiz Kids

It was not only in Australia that players and officials became conscious of tactical changes in the game. Reliance on a sound back court game as the foundation of a successful attack from the net was soon superseded by the Big Game, where reliance on the serve and volley was all important. While the Australians, under Captain Harry Hopman's tutelage, were the first to succeed in overcoming the American holders of the Davis Cup, players all over the world were abandoning the time-tried fundamentals for the new hit and run tactics.

In Europe, Jaroslav Drobny and Vladimir Cernik of Czechoslovakia in 1946, Tony Mottram and Geoff Paish of Great Britain in 1947, Kurt Nielsen and Torben Ulrich of Denmark in 1948, Philippe Washer and Jackie Brichant of Belgium in 1949, and Sven Davidson of Sweden in 1950 all came to the front by concentrating on the serve and volley game.

There was an entry of 21 nations in the European Zone in 1951, with 5 in the American Zone.

As a foretaste of future events, the new American Champion, Art Larsen, was invited to visit Australia. Dick Savitt accompanied him. Larsen beat Frank Sedgman at Sydney and lost to him at Melbourne. Savitt took the big one when he beat Ken McGregor to become the first American winner of the Australian title since Don Budge in 1938. From Australia Savitt went to Egypt, the Rivera and the Italian and French Championships. At Wimbledon he won his second major title. In the final he again met McGregor and repeated his Australian win. At Forest Hills he had a painful infection in his leg and lost to Vic Seixas. Sedgman beat Larsen in the semi-final and Seixas in the final.

With Gottfried von Cramm coming back from the shadows, Germany put up a strong team in the Davis Cup and reached the final. In their first match, von Cramm beat both Mitic and Branovic of Yugoslavia and, with Goepfert, beat Mitic and Palada in doubles. Wins over Denmark (4-1), Belgium (3-2), and Italy (3-2) followed. In the final at Bastad, the Swedes proved too strong and only lost two sets for a 5-0 win.

In the American Zone, the United States beat Japan, Mexico and Canada without losing a rubber. Different combinations were tried out and the team which was sent to Australia with Frank Shields as Captain included Dick Savitt, Vic Seixas, Ted Schroeder, Tony Trabert and Ham Richardson. Trabert and Schroeder played all five rubbers against the Swedes at Melbourne and won them all. To Savitt's bitter disappointment, Shields passed him and named Schroeder and Seixas for the Challenge Round, with Schroeder-Trabert for the Doubles. Captain Hopman named Mervyn Rose as his second singles player. Rose lost both his matches. Sedgman, as expected, won both of his. The unbeaten doubles team of Sedgman-McGregor made the final score 3-2 for Australia. There was a bitter debate at the Annual Meeting of the USLTA when Seixas was ranked No. 1 ahead of Savitt, who had won the Australian and Wimbledon singles. Shields justified his choice in a strong criticism of Savitt's lack of cooperation.

In 1952 it was McGregor's turn to win the Australian Championships. Australian dominance continued right through the year as Sedgman won both the Italian and Wimbledon titles. At Longwood Sedgman-McGregor were upset by the pick-up team of Seixas and Rose, but at Forest Hills Sedgman beat Gar Mulloy in the final, completing a run of straight-set victories.

Twenty-two nations challenged in the European Zone of the Davis Cup the next year, and Belgium, France, Italy and Denmark came through to the semi-finals. France was still searching for a winning combination and lost to the Belgians at Paris. Italy still depended on Gianni Cucelli and the del Bellos, with a new and completely unorthodox player, Fausto Gardini, as the second singles player. In the quarter-finals, France beat Argentina, Belgium defeated Sweden, Italy beat Great Britain and Denmark beat Germany. Von Cramm had now retired. Belgium beat France and Italy beat Denmark in the semi-final, and Italy won the European Zone final three rubbers to one. India had no competition in the Eastern Zone but lost to Italy in the first interzone tie at Brisbane.

There were only three challengers besides America in the American Zone, and the United States team lost only one match when Brendan Macken of Canada beat Bob Perry in the final. Eight different players were on the teams which beat Japan, Mexico and Canada, and Vic Seixas was named to Captain the team which was sent to Australia. Tony Trabert obtained leave from the Navy to join the team, and Ham Richardson and Straight Clark accompanied Seixas on his mission. At Sydney, the Italians were beaten 5-0.

There had been strong competition in the chase for Sedgman's signature on a professional contract, and it was only by giving him a substantial wedding present that the Australian LTA had been able to keep him "pure" in 1951. Now, when he and McGregor once more had safely retained the Cup, they both signed with Jack Kramer. This caused great consternation in Australia but Hopman was calm. He felt sure his Whiz Kids, Ken Rosewall and Lew Hoad, could still hold the Cup.

Rosewall drew first blood by winning the Australian Championships in January, 1953. The touring team, under Hopman's command, proceeded to France where Rosewall won the French title. Seixas had beaten Hoad in the semi-finals but succumbed to the "Little Master" in the final. The Whiz Kids won the doubles from another Australian pair. At Wimbledon, the surprise of the tournament was Kurt Nielsen of Denmark who, unseeded, beat Gar Mulloy, Ken Rosewall and Jaroslav Drobny to reach the final. Here he met Vic Seixas, who had come through with wins over three other Australians—George Worthington, Lew Hoad and Mervyn Rose—and he lost to the American in four sets.

There were 22 nations in the Davis Cup European Zone and six in the American, besides India, winner in the Asian Zone.

Denmark, France, Belgium and Italy reached the semi-finals of the European Zone. Nielsen and Torben Ulrich played all rive rubbers for the Danes, and Paul Remy's win over Ulrich was the only French point. Beppe Merlo had joined Gardini as the second singles player for Italy, with the veteran doubles team of Cucelli and Bel Bello completing the side. Merlo beat Jackie Brichant in five sets and the Italians won the doubles, the final score being three rubbers to two for Belgium. In the final, played at Copenhagen, the Belgians won the European title by three rubbers to two.

Mario Llamas and Pancho Contreras were new members of the Mexican team which lost to the Canadians at Montreal by 3 rubbers to 2. Tony Trabert, Ham Richardson and Tom Brown beat the Japanese team of Kosei Kamo and Atsushi Miyagi at Vancouver 5-0. Canada beat Cuba 3-2 in one semi-final, and Gar Mulloy, Tut Bartzen and Bob Perry beat the West Indies at Kingston, Jamaica, 5-0. In the final, played at Montreal, Seixas, Trabert and Straight Clark beat the Canadians with the loss of only two sets.

The Interzone final in Australia brought together Belgium and India at Perth. A young Indian, Ramanathan Krishnan, joined the veteran Misra for this rubber and won the first two sets from Jackie Brichant on the third day.

Bill Talbert, winner of the National Doubles with Mulloy for four years, had been appointed Captain of the United States team. He had also won the the French Doubles with Trabert in 1950. He chose the same team—Seixas and Trabert—to meet the Belgians in the Interzone final. The result was a 4-1 win, Seixas losing to Brichant in four sets.

When the American team moved on to Melbourne for the Challenge Round, it had high hopes for victory. In the American Championships at Forest Hills the semi-finals had brought together the two Davis Cup pairs. Seixas had repeated his Wimbledon win over Hoad and Trabert had given Rosewall a lesson. But the draw at Melbourne was unfavorable to the Americans. Seixas lost to Hoad in the opening match 6-4, 6-2, 6-3. Then Trabert evened the score with another win over Rosewall 6-3, 6-4, 6-4. Hopman believed that Rex Hartwig would be a stronger partner than Rosewall for Hoad in the doubles, but they proved to be an ill-assorted pair and Trabert and Seixas beat them in straight sets 6-2, 6-4, 6-4. The Americans now led 2 rubbers to 1. On the third day, in a drizzle, Hoad won the first set against Trabert 13-11 and the second 6-3. Tony changed to spikes and won the third at 6-2 and the fourth at 6-4 to even the score. The fifth set was a battle of services in which each player had chances for a break. The end came in the twelfth game with Trabert serving with new balls. Hoad, with the odd game to his credit, went out for his shots and took the deciding game at love. The score was now tied at two matches each.

With the rain still pouring down, the deciding match was postponed until the next day. Rosewall got into his stride first and broke service to lead 3-1. He held his own thereafter and took the first set 6-2. Seixas increased the pressure and, volleying brilliantly, won the second, also at 6-2. There were several questionable line decisions in the third set which upset Seixas, who dropped his service in the fourth game and lost the set at 6-3. After the intermission, Rosewall attacked from the start and won a vital break in the first game. Games then went with service until Rosewall earned another break to give him a lead of 5-3 with his own service to follow. He continued to 40-15 in the ninth game but Seixas made a great stand, won the game and needed only two points to even the score at 5-all. But it was not to be. Rosewall pulled up to deuce, then won the game for the set at 6-4.

The first major championship of 1954, in Australia, was won by Mervyn Rose who beat Rex Hartwig in four sets in the final. Nevertheless, there was no thought of replacing the Whiz Kids on the defending Davis Cup team. Nor was there any thought in America of replacing Billy Talbert as the American Captain.

A foretaste of things to come occurred at Paris when only one of the Australians reached the quarter-final. Tony Trabert, Budge Patty, and Art

Ken Rosewall. (Courtesy *World Tennis)*

Larsen of United States and Enrique Morea of Argentina were the semi-finalists. Trabert and Larsen came through to the final, and Tony beat Art in straight sets for the title. At Wimbledon it was the old campaigner, Jaroslav Drobny, who came through in a surprise win. Seeded only eleventh, the former Czech, now an Egyptian citizen, was out to show up the committee. Drob beat Lew Hoad in the quarters, Patty in the semi-finals and Rosewall in four sets in the final. Seixas lost to Patty in the quarters and Trabert was beaten by Rosewall in the semis. Hartwig and Rose won the doubles over Seixas-Trabert, who had put out Hoad–Rosewall in the semi-final at 8-6 in the fifth set.

At Forest Hills, Trabert lost to Hartwig and Hoad to Ham Richardson. Hartwig beat Rosewall in the semi-final and met Seixas for the title. Vic won his only American Championship in four sets.

The American team for the Challenge Round, captained for the second year by Billy Talbert, was Seixas, Trabert, Richardson and Mike Green, a young player sent along for experience. Sweden, with Lennart Bergelin, Sven Davidson and Torsten Johansson, won the European Zone, beating France five rubbers to none in the final. In the Interzone Final, played at Brisbane, the Swedes did not win a match from the Americans, who had beaten the West Indies, Cuba and Mexico with the loss of only one rubber.

In preparing for the Challenge Round, Talbert devised a plan for Seixas to turn the tables on his nemesis, Rosewall. Instead of hitting his first service hard and rushing for the net position, Vic was to advance only after a strong forcing shot to Ken's forehand. When Hoad and Trabert met in the first match, a long and exciting struggle was looked for. But Hoad made many errors in the gusty arena and Trabert won handily. Following Talbert's plan to the letter, Seixas then proceeded to beat Rosewall 8-6, 6-8, 6-4, 6-3. The Americans were two up. Now Hopman was on the spot. Hartwig and Hoad had not hit it off too well the previous year, so Hopman went back to his former combination of Hoad and Rosewall. Once again the Americans used the signal system which had been successful in 1953. Again it disconcerted the Australian pair. At the end of the day the United States had already won back the Cup. With the pressure off, the Americans had no incentive to go all out. The final score was 3-2. A great celebration welcomed the victorious team when they arrived home with the treasured Cup.

19

Peru Contributes to a U. S. Win

Shortly after the victorious American Davis Cup team returned home in the early days of 1955 a welcoming celebration greeted them. A dinner in their honor was held at the Seventh Regiment Tennis Club rooms in the armory on Park Avenue in New York. Officers and Executive Committee members of the USLTA, City and State personalities were present, and speeches praising the accomplishment of the team mingled with toasts in champagne ladled from the Cup on the center of the head table. "Uncle Mike" Myrick was prevailed upon without much trouble to sing his famous song "And Let the Rest of the World Go By," and speeches were made by Captain Talbert, Vic Seixas and Tony Trabert who had performed the miracle. In Australia there were no recriminations, only a resolve not to let it happen again.

With the change in the Champion Nation, as had happened before, there was an increase in the number of Challengers for the 1955 contest. Twenty-four nations challenged in the European Zone, three in the Eastern Zone and six, including Australia, in the American. Among the newer faces on the challenging teams were Enrique Morea of Argentine, Gordon Forbes and Abe Segal of South Africa, Luis Ayala of Chile, Robert Haillet of France, Ulf Schmidt of Sweden, Nicola Pietrangeli and Orlando Sirola of Italy, Billy Knight of Great Britain, Felicissimo Ampon and Reymundo Deyro of the Philippines, Esteban Reyes of Mexico, and Bob Falkenburg, winner of the Wimbledon Title in 1948 as an American, now playing for his adopted country, Brazil.

Despite their loss of the Cup, the Australians had not lost confidence in their ability to rise to the top again. In addition to the Whiz Kids, Harry Hopman was busy grooming another group of youngsters to replace them if need be. Among them were Ashley Cooper and Roy Emerson, both eighteen, Malcolm Anderson, twenty; and Neale Fraser, twenty-one. All these players, along with Lew Hoad, Ken Rosewall, Mervyn Rose and Rex Hartwig, were entered in the Wimbledon Championships in 1954.

In January, 1955, Rosewall won his second Australian Championship, beating Hoad in the final. The Australians saved their energies for the big events to come and did not enter the Italian or French Championships. Tony Trabert repeated his win of the French Championships and again won the doubles with Vic Seixas. The semi-finalists at Wimbledon were Rosewall and Kurt Nielsen, Budge Patty and Trabert. Hoad had lost to Patty in straight sets in the quarters and Vic Seixas was upset by Gil Shea of California in the third round. Nielsen and Trabert met in the final, with Trabert the winner in straight sets.

The Davis Cup contest in the European Zone had meanwhile progressed to the semi-finals. Fausto Gardini, Nicola Pietrangeli and Orlando Sirola of Italy defeated the British team of Roger Becker, Billy Knight, Mike Davies and Bobby Wilson 5-0. The Swedish team of Sven Davidson, Lennart Bergelin and Torsten Johansson beat the Chileans, Luis Ayala and Andres Hammersley, 3-2 at Bastaad. In the final, played at Milan, the Italians qualified for the Interzones by 4 rubbers to 1.

In the American Zone, Australia beat Mexico at Chicago 5-0 while Brazil beat Cuba 4-1. The Aussies defeated Brazil in the second round 4-1, Canada in the final at Montreal 5-0; Japan 4-0; and Italy in the Interzone at Philadelphia 5-0.

The Challenge Round was played at Forest Hills before the Championships and, in view of the results of the previous year and Trabert's sensational play through the season, a repeat of the Americans' supremacy was looked for. Rosewall met Seixas in the first rubber but the result did not follow the pattern of 1954. The little Australian won in four sets. Hoad beat Talbert almost as easily and, when Hoad and Hartwig beat Seixas and Trabert at 7-5 in the fifth set, the Cup was on its way back to Australia for another three years.

In the American Championships which followed, Trabert won his third major title of the year. He beat Hoad in the semi-final and Rosewall in the final. Despite his poor showing in the Davis Cup, Tony was unquestionably the player of the year and won the usual reward of a contract to play as a professional. Jack Kramer tried to sign Rosewall and Hoad too, and although they expressed interest they were dissuaded when they returned home. The Americans had lost the mainstay of their Davis Cup team.

Twenty-four nations challenged in the European Zone in 1956, three in the Eastern Zone and five in the American. Italy, France, Sweden and Great Britain came through to the semi-finals before Wimbledon. Hoad had won the Australian and French titles, and he and Rosewall were in the Wimbledon semi-finals, along with Seixas and Ham Richardson. Hoad beat Richardson in four sets and Seixas once more succumbed to Rosewall's mastery in five. Hoad was the winner in the final. He now had three of the four major titles for a grand slam.

Following Wimbledon, Italy beat France in one Davis Cup semi-final by three rubbers to two, while Sweden beat Great Britain at Stockholm 4-1. In the Eastern Zone, India beat Japan 3-2; in the American Zone, the United States beat Canada and Mexico 4-1 in each tie. The Interzone Final was played at Forest Hills and the United States beat Italy 4-1.

In the United States Championships, Hoad and Rosewall won the doubles and at Forest Hills they reached the final. But the "Little Master" spoiled his teammate's bid for the Grand Slam by beating him in four sets.

Ham Richardson was chosen to accompany Seixas to Australia but was unable to go. Herb Flam was selected in his place. Billy Talbert again captained the team, and Mike Green and Sam Giammalva were also sent along. India was beaten at Perth but the Challenge Round was a 5-0 rout. Soon thereafter Rosewall signed with Kramer as a professional. Hoad was also tempted but decided to have one more try at the "Grand Slam." This did not unduly discourage Hopman especially when, with Hoad on the sidelines, Ashley Cooper beat Neale Fraser in the final of the 1957 Australian Championships.

A dozen Australian players, with Hopman in charge, were sent overseas, and the surprise of the French Championships was the defeat of Hoad in the second round by his compatriot, Neil Gibson. Cooper, Fraser and Rose reached the quarters, but the finalists were Sven Davidson and Herb Flam, with Davidson taking the title in straight sets.

In the Davis Cup there were twenty-four entries in the European Zone, including Mexico, New Zealand, South Africa and Chile from overseas; five in the Eastern Zone, and seven, including Israel, in the American. The European quarter-finalists were Belgium, Mexico, Great Britain, France, Sweden, Denmark, Italy and Poland. Jackie Brichant and Philippe Washer of Belgium beat Mario Llamas and Pancho Contreras at Brussels 3-2, then beat Mike Davies and Bobby Wilson of Great Britain, also 3-2. Sweden won over Denmark and Italy defeated Poland 4-1. The finalists were Belgium and Italy and the Belgians won 3-2. Japan lost to the Philippines at Manila 3-2. The United States won the American Zone title, beating the British West Indies, Venezuela and Brazil with the loss of only one rubber.

At Wimbledon, four Australians – Ashley Cooper, Neale Fraser, Mervyn Rose and Lew Hoad – reached the quarter-finals, along with Seixas and Flam of the United States and Schmidt and Davidson of Sweden. Cooper and Hoad met in the final, with Hoad the winner in straight sets with the

Alex Olmedo, the Peruvian who helped bring the Davis Cup back to America. (Courtesy *World Tennis)*

loss of only five games. The applause had hardly died down when Hoad signed Kramer's contract and became a professional. Even after Hoad's departure, the Australians were able to put up a strong front. Cooper and Fraser won the American Doubles and Mal Anderson beat Cooper in the final of the Singles at Forest Hills.

With Ham Richardson again unavailable, the Americans had to count on the veterans, Vic Seixas and Herb Flam, along with young Barry MacKay,Intercollegiate Champion from the University of Michigan. Hopman named Cooper and Anderson for the singles and Anderson and Rose for the doubles. At Brisbane the United States beat Belgium in the Interzone final three rubbers to two, but at Melbourne Cooper beat Seixas and Anderson beat MacKay, both in five sets. When Anderson and Rose won the doubles in straight sets, Austrailia had once more successfully defended its title.

The continued successes of the Australians in spite of the defection of their leading players to the professionals caused a revolt in the American administration. Up to this time leadership of the USLTA had resided in the East, although for several years playing strength had come from the Western half of the country. Spurred by a costly celebration of the Association's 75th Anniversary, the nominating committee, at the 1958 Annual Meeting, selected a slate of Middle Western, Far Western and Southern officers whose first action was to replace Billy Talbert (an Easterner) as Captain of the Davis Cup team with Perry T. Jones of Los Angeles, a capable administrator but an unknown quantity at courtside.

In preparing to recapture the Cup, Jones announced that he had engaged Jack Kramer as coach of the team and that one of the players he had in mind was a Peruvian lad, Alex Olmedo. Alex was a student at the University of Southern California and he had won the Intercollegiate singles and doubles championships in 1956 and again in 1958. A great furor arose when these plans leaked out, but there was no question that Olmedo was eligible as he had never represented his native country in Davis Cup competition.

In Australia Ashley Cooper beat Mal Anderson in the Championships. Cooper-Fraser won the doubles. Mervyn Rose took both the Italian and French titles. It seemed as though the supply of champions in Australia was unlimited.

Sixteen nations challenged in the Davis Cup European Zone in 1958, plus the eight exempt nations. In addition there were five in the Eastern Zone and seven in the American, a total of thirty-six. India challenged in Europe and lost to Italy in the second round. Brazil and Chile also challenged in Europe and both lost their second matches – Brazil to Great

Britain and Chile to France. Mexico was one of the exempted nations but lost to Poland 3-2 in the quarter-finals. The four semi-finalists were Poland, Italy, Great Britain and France. The Philippines beat Ceylon in the Eastern Zone and the United States defeated Venezuela, Canada and Argentina for the American Zone title.

At Wimbledon Cooper and Fraser were the finalists. Cooper again beat his teammate, but they lost the doubles to Sven Davidson and Ulf Schmidt of Sweden. In America, Barry MacKay beat Alex Olmedo at Merion. Ham Richardson won at Southampton. Mal Anderson was the winner at Orange and Newport. In the National Doubles, Olmedo and Richardson teamed for the first time. They beat Cooper-Fraser in four sets in the semi-final and the second American pair, Giammalva-MacKay, in the final. At Forest Hills none of the Americans reached the semi-finals. When Cooper met Anderson again for the title, the 1957 result was reversed. In spite of a damaging fall, Cooper scored a sensational five-set win.

During the Championships, Captain Jones named a Davis Cup squad which included Olmedo. There was quite a furor over his appointment but Jones stuck to his guns. Richardson, MacKay and two young players, Butch Buchholz and Chris Crawford, accompanied Olmedo and Jones to Australia. The Italians defeated the Philippines at Sydney 5-0 and met the American team at Perth. MacKay took Richardson's place on the third day, and the final result was a 5-0 win for the Americans.

When the team arrived in Brisbane for the Challenge Round, it was learned that Richardson, America's No. 1 player and winner over Olmedo at Los Angeles, had been named only for the doubles. Olmedo and MacKay were to play the singles. Although Richardson resented the implied slight, he resolved to do his part.

Olmedo met Anderson in the opening match and won 8-6, 2-6, 9-7, 8-6. Cooper beat MacKay 4-6, 6-3, 6-2, 6-4. The doubles between Olmedo-Richardson and Anderson-Fraser was the longest doubles match in Davis Cup history. The Americans were down two sets to none, 10-12, 3-6, and two match points, but came back to win the next three 16-14, 6-3, 7-5, a total of eighty-two games. On the third day, Olmedo beat Cooper 6-3, 4-6, 6-4, 8-6 for the deciding point. MacKay's loss to Anderson in the final rubber was of no account.

Following the usual pattern, Cooper and Anderson had already been approached by Kramer and signed with him to become professionals. America's road to a prolonged holding of the Cup seemed clear.

20

Quick Turnabout

The American champions returned from Australia after winning the 1958 Challenge Round and received a tumultuous welcome in Los Angeles and all across the continent. They were Alex Olmedo, Ham Richardson and Barry MacKay. Peru was not forgotten and Captain Perry Jones accompanied Olmedo on a visit to his fatherland. At the Annual Meeting of USLTA, President Denny reappointed Jones to lead the team in its first defense of the Cup.

Olmedo had confirmed his standing by winning the Australian Championship and Aussies Ashley Cooper and Mal Anderson had followed the usual pattern by enlisting in Jack Kramer's troupe as professionals. Though Neale Fraser remained an amateur and a young player named Rodney Laver showed signs of becoming Aussie Captain Harry Hopman's choice for the next Australian Cup team, Jones and the American officials had no misgivings. Olmedo won the U. S. Indoor title, then five months later took the Wimbledon crown.

Twenty-four nations challenged for the Davis Cup in the European Zone, eight in the Eastern Zone, three in the North American and four in the South American—a total of thirty-nine competitors plus the holding nation, the United States. France, Italy, Poland and Great Britain were seeded in Europe and, of these, Poland lost its opening tie to Brazil. Two rounds were played before the French Championships and the third round was completed before Wimbledon. France beat Roumania at Paris 5-0; Italy beat South Africa at Florence 4-1, Abe Segal's win over Orlando Sirola being South Africa's only point; Spain beat Brazil at Barcelona, 4-1, the doubles going to Carlos Fernandes-Ronnie Barnes in four sets; and Great Britain beat Chile at Eastbourne 3-2, Bobby Wilson's win over Patricio Rodriguez on the final day being the deciding point. Following Wimbledon, Italy met France in the semi-finals. Nicola Pietrangeli and Sirola beat Pierre Darmon and Robert Haillet on the first day and teamed to clinch the tie by downing Jean Noel Grinda and Darmon in straight sets in the doubles. Great Britain and Spain had a close match in the other semi-finals at Barcelona. Manuel Santana's win over Mike Davies at five sets in the final rubber gave Spain the tie. The final, played at Milan, went to Italy by 4 rubbers to 1, Gimeno's victory over Tacchini on the last day being Spain's only point.

Olmedo and MacKay headed the American contingent at Wimbledon. MacKay beat Neale Fraser, then lost to Laver in one semi-final. Olmedo came through without trouble and beat Laver in the final to win the crown.

The Australians hurried to Mexico for their first Davis Cup tie. The result was much closer than the 4-1 score, although Mexico's only victory came when Mario Llamas beat Laver. All the other singles matches were cliff-hangers. Canada and Cuba were beaten. In the Interzone final Laver lost another match to Ramanathan Krishnan of India.

The Americans returned from Wimbledon in time for the National Clay Court Championships. Olmedo and MacKay made a sorry showing. Olmedo was beaten again at Merion. Jones picked Olmedo to team with Butch Buchholz and they won at Merion and Orange. At Longwood the American and Australian pairs met in the final. The Australians won in five sets.

When the teams met at Forest Hills in the Challenge Round, it was Fraser insead of Olmedo who was the hero of the tie. His fine, all-round game was too much for the hesitant Peruvian in the opening match. MacKay beat Laver in the second. The doubles, which might have gone either way, was no contest, with Roy Emerson playing a stellar role. Olmedo tied the score on the third day with a victory over Laver. But MacKay could not repeat his Wimbledon win over Fraser. After the match was postponed at set-all Fraser won the final two sets handily. Once more the Cup returned to Australia.

The Championships were marked by Fraser's continued brilliance. MacKay was beaten by "Tut" Bartzen, a clay court specialist from Texas. Olmedo and Fraser met once more in the final. Though Alex was suffering from a strained shoulder, it is doubtful if, even in his best form, he could have defeated the handsome Australian who had played second fiddle for so long—first to Hoad and Rosewall, then to Cooper and Anderson.

At the annual meeting of the USLTA in January, 1960, there was another shuffle of officers. George Barnes of Chicago moved up to the presidency. He appointed David Freed of Salt Lake City, Utah, to be Davis Cup Captain, with Tut Bartzen as his assistant. Olmedo, notwithstanding his comedown, joined Kramer's galaxy of stars. Freed had to get together a new Davis Cup team, built around MacKay and Buchholz. The Australians, with Fraser, Laver, Emerson and a new crop of

Neale Fraser. (Courtesy *World Tennis)*

youngsters, could stand pat.

It was not Fraser but Laver who won the 1960 Australian Championships. Fraser-Emerson lost to Laver-Bob Mark in the doubles. Fraser and Emerson came to America and played in the Indoor Championships and on the Caribbean Circuit with only moderate success. MacKay won the Indoors. When he and Fraser met in Texas in the spring, Barry was again the winner.

Twenty-four nations entered the European Zone Davis Cup draw, with the four 1959 semi-finalists seeded. These were Spain, France, Great Britain and Italy. Six entries in the Pacific Zone and the same number in the American Zone brought the total entries to thirty-six. In the Eastern Zone, played early in the spring, the Philippines beat Japan 3-2 in one semi-final while India beat Thailand in the other. In the final, the Philippines surprisingly had a 5-0 victory over India.

In Europe, two rounds were played before the French Championships with one of the seeds, Spain, falling to Sweden 3 rubbers to 2.

MacKay went to Europe and won the Italian Championships on the basis of his big serve and volley game (even on clay). At Paris, Pietrangeli repeated his 1959 win. At Wimbledon Fraser and MacKay were seeded one and two. In the quarter-finals, Pietrangeli beat MacKay, Laver downed Emerson and Krishnan won over Luis Ayala. Fraser beat Buchholz after the young American had a lead of two sets to one and three match points in the fourth. In this set, which went to 15-all, Buchholz fell and twisted his ankle. On resuming play he was seized with cramp and collapsed. The final brought together the two Australians. This time Fraser realized his long time ambition when he beat Laver.

In the Davis Cup quarter-finals, Sweden beat Germany at Dusseldorf, Christian Kuhnke's win over Ulf Schmidt being the only German point. France downed Denmark at Paris 5-0, Great Britain shut out Belgium at Scarborough and Italy squeezed passed Chile 3-2 at Turin (Ayala won both his matches but Pietrangeli and Sirola won in straight sets in the doubles), Sweden and Italy came through to the final, Sweden over France 3-2 and Italy over Britain 4-1. In the final, played at Bastaad on July 31 to August 2, Pietrangeli and Sirola's win of the doubles at 14-16, 5-7, 6-2, 6-3, 6-2 was the deciding point. Italy again won the European Zone.

While Fraser and Emerson remained in Europe, the rest of the Australian team entered the American Clay Court Championships. Bartzen beat Laver but lost to MacKay in the final. Laver then won four grass court events—at Merion, Southampton, Orange and Newport while MacKay, Bartzen and the new doubles pair of Buchholz and Chuck McKinley were engaged in Davis Cup ties against Canada, Mexico and Venezuela. Emerson and Fraser arrived in time to win the National Doubles at Longwood.

At Forest Hills, MacKay was beaten by Bob Mark. Emerson lost to Ham Richardson. Dennis Ralston, winner of the Wimbledon Doubles with Rafael Osuna of Mexico, beat Mark. The semi-finalists were Fraser, Ralston, Laver and Buchholz. The seventeen-year old Ralston put up a good fight against Fraser. He carried the first set to 11-9 before the Australian's big service proved too much for him. Buchholz gained a two sets to none lead on Laver, dropped the third and fourth and was leading 5-3 with his service to follow when the cramps which had beset him at Wimbledon again caused him to falter. Laver took the ninth game but Buchholz had three match points in the tenth before Laver pulled out to even the count at 5-all. At 30-love in the 11th game, Buchholz was through. He fell to the court in agony, was massaged and resumed play. He went through the motions but his mobility had vanished. It was Laver's third final of the year against Fraser. This time Fraser's superiority left no doubt.

Fraser and Emerson were called home by their Association as they had overstayed their alloted time out of the country. The rest of the Australians entered the Pacific Southwest tournament at Los Angeles. MacKay and Buchholz met in the final with Barry the winner. Buchholz and McKinley won the doubles. MacKay followed this victory with another win in the Pacific Coast.

Shortly after, the American Davis Cup team—MacKay, Buchholz, McKinley and Ralston, with Captain Freed and Assistant Captain Bartzen—flew to Australia. In the first Interzone tie they had a 5-0 win over Philippines, but in the final, when they met the Italian team at Perth, disaster overtook them. After winning the first two singles, the Americans lost the doubles and Buchholz's loss to Pietrangeli tied the score at two rubbers apiece. Then Sirola, not generally considered in MacKay's class and his victim the previous summer at Rome, dealt the finishing blow in straight sets.

This victory placed a European team in the Challenge Round for the first time since 1937. But the invincible Australians, Fraser, Laver and Emerson, with Hopman directing their strategy, had an easy 4-1 victory over the Italians for their ninth win of the Cup in the past eleven years.

There were 42 challenges for the Cup in 1961; the usual 28 in the European, 7 in the Eastern and 7 in the American Zone. It might be noted that Chile, Brazil, the United Arab Republic, South Africa, Turkey, New Zealand and Israel entered in the European Zone and Morocco in the American. Italy, France, Great Britain and Sweden were seeded in Europe and succeeded in reaching the semi-final as expected. Italy, France, West Germany, Poland, South Africa, Great Britain, Spain and Sweden reached the quarter-final round. Among the surprises were Jackie Brichant's wins for Belgium over both Pietrangeli and Sirola and Franz Saiko of Austria's win over Bobby Wilson of England.

Laver, Emerson and Fraser came to America in time to take part in the Florida-Caribbean Circuit. Of the ten tournaments, Emerson and Laver each won three and were runners-up in two others. In the Italian Championships Pietrangeli beat Laver in the final and at Paris it was Santana who came through, beating Mike Sangster of England, Emerson, Laver and Pietrangeli. Another round of the Davis Cup saw Italy the winner over West Germany, France the victor over Poland, Great Britain conqueror of South Africa and Sweden the surprise winner over Spain.

At Wimbledon, another of the long line of Australians came to the top. Fraser, the defending champion, fell to Bobby Wilson of England in the fourth round in four sets, but Rod the "Rocket" Laver beat Krishnan of India in one semi-final while McKinley beat Sangster of England in the other. Laver had an easy time in the final, 6-3, 6-1, 6-4.

Italy and Sweden were finalists in the Davis Cup European Zone and Italy won by four rubbers to one. India came through in the Eastern Zone, beating Japan in the final. The United States beat Mexico in a very close match in the American Zone.

The regulations for the Interzone finals were changed at the meeting of the Davis Cup nations in July, necessitating the journey of the American team, first to India at New Delhi, then to Rome to meet the Italians. As both ties would be played on clay, Captain Freed was counting on Bartzen for one of the singles. But Tut could not make the trip and McKinley, Whitney Reed, Donald Dell and Marty Riessen were taken to New Delhi where the Indians were beaten narrowly, Ramanathan Krishnan winning both his matches.

Following this match, McKinley was called home to his studies and Jon Douglas went to Rome to take his place against the Italians. On the first day Douglas won his match against Fausto Gardini and Reed was leading Pietrangeli two sets to none and 3-4 in the third when the match was called on account of darkness. On the next day Pietrangeli pulled it out in the fifth set. The doubles went to Pietrangeli-Sirola and the tie was won by Italy when Pietrangeli beat Douglas in the first match on the final day. Reed then lost to Gardini to give the Italians a 4-1 victory.

Gardini refused to go to Australia unless he was assured of a singles berth, so Pietrangeli and Sirola played all five matches for the challengers. It was another five-love win for the holders. In the Kooyong Stadium at Melbourne, Emerson beat Pietrangeli 8-6, 6-4, 6-0, Laver beat Sirola 6-1, 6-4, 6-3, Fraser-Emerson beat Pietrangeli-Sirola 6-2, 6-3, 6-4, Laver beat Pietrangeli 6-3, 3-6, 4-6, 6-3, 8-6 and Emerson beat Sirola 6-3, 6-3, 4-6, 6-2.

21

For One Year Only

The year 1962 was chiefly noteworthy for the appearance of a new "Grand Slam" winner – Rodney G. Laver of Australia – and a new Davis Cup Challenger, Mexico.

Laver, who had been coming to the fore as the successor to his compatriots Sedgman, Hoad, Cooper and Fraser, accomplished the feat of winning the four major singles Championships – Australia, France, Great Britain and America –in one year, which had remained unequalled since Don Budge's triumph in 1938.

There were several European and Asian players in the Australian Championships at Sydney, but only Wilhelm Bungert of Germany reached the quarter-finals. Laver, Bob Hewitt, Roy Emerson and Neale Fraser were the semi-finalists, and in the final Laver beat Emerson 8-6, 0-6, 6-4, 6-4. Laver then went to America where Chuck McKinley beat him in the semi-final of the U. S. Indoor Championships. Roy Emerson joined Laver for the Caribbean Circuit in which Manuel Santana of Spain and Mike Sangster of England, among others, also took part.

Once more 28 nations entered the European Zone Davis Cup lists, with Sweden, France, Great Britain and Italy exempt from the first round. There were eight entries in the Eastern Zone and only five in the American, including Yugoslavia, a European nation.

The Eastern Zone, as usual, was the first completed. Iran, India, Japan and Philippines were the semi-finalists and India was the winner over Iran and Philippines, with Jaidip Mukerjea, Premjit Lall and Ramanathan Krishnan comprising the Indian side.

In the European Zone the first two rounds were played, as usual, before the French Championships at the end of May. Chile and New Zealand of the non-European nations lost in the first round, but South Africa beat France and Brazil beat Poland to reach the third round. The Australians appeared in force for the Italian Championships in Rome and the French Championships at Paris, and Laver proceeded on his way to the Grand

Slam by winning both. Emerson was his opponent in the Italian final and again at Paris.

The quarter-finalists for the Davis Cup played their matches during the week-end of June 16. England defeated Brazil at Eastbourne 4-1, with Mike Sangster and Billy Knight taking both their singles while Edson Mandarino and Ronnie Barnes won a point for Brazil by winning the doubles from Knight and Tony Pickard. Ulf Schmidt and Jan Erik Lundquist won a 5-0 victory over Czechoslovakia, Istvan Gulyas of Hungary beat Nicki Pietrangeli, but Italy won the other four matches. The cloest tie was played in Berlin when the South African team of Cliff Drysdale, Gordon Forbes and Abe Segal beat Ingo Buding, Wihelm Bungert and Christian Kuhnke of West Germany 3 rubbers to 2.

Laver won the third jewel for his crown at Wimbledon where the quarter-finalists, in addition to Laver, were Manuel Santana, Rafael Osuna, and five other Australians.

The Davis Cup semi-finals pitted the Italian team of Pietrangeli, Fausto Gardini and Orlando Sirola against the British team of Sangster, Knight and Pickard at Milan, and the British won only three sets in losing 5-0. Sweden played South Africa at Bastaad and Drysdale's win over Schmidt was the only point for the Springboks. Two weeks later, the Swedes became European Zone titlists with a 4-1 win over Italy.

In the American Zone, the United States defeated Canada 5-0 in July and then met Mexico in Mexico City early in August. President Ed Turville of the USLTA had chosen a new Captain to replace David Freed. Bob Kelleher, a veteran player from Southern California, selected Chuck McKinley and Jack Douglas for the singles and McKinley and Dennis Ralston for the doubles. This was the team which beat Canada in the preceding round and was expected to down the Mexican team of Osuna and Antonio Palafox handily. McKinley did all he could when he won both his matches but Douglas, who was counted on to defeat Palafox in the second singles, lost in four sets. In the doubles Ralston served no less than 18 double faults so that, after leading two sets to one at the intermission, the Americans lost the next two 6-3, 6-2. Osuna then completed the Mexican victory by beating Douglas at 6-1 in the fifth set.

This placed the Mexican team in the Interzone final and Sweden came to Mexico City for the match. As had happened before, the visiting team found the altitude too much for them and Mexico won the match 4 rubbers to 1. This necessitated the Mexicans traveling to India for the final Interzone match. Though the conditions in India favored the home players, Mexico won the tie 4-1 and met Australia in the Challenge Round at Brisbane in December. Laver beat Osuna 6-2, 6-1, 7-5; Fraser beat

Palafox 7-9, 6-3, 6-4, 11-9; Emerson and Laver won the doubles 7-5, 6-2, 6-4; Fraser beat Osuna 3-6, 11-9, 6-1, 3-6, 6-4 and Laver beat Palafox 6-1, 4-6, 6-4, 8-6, thus completing another sweep and Laver's "Grand Slam" of the major championships.

The cheers for "Rocket Rod's" feat had hardly died down when he placed his signature on a professional contract. With his departure from the amateur ranks, interest in the Davis Cup again reached fever heat. The United States was determined not to repeat its mistakes of the last three years and Kelleher, who was reappointed Captain of the American team, vowed that he would lead it to victory this time. Mexico, whose champion Osuna was the United States singles title holder, was determined to have another go at the crown. Other Latin-American countries, besides those of Europe and South America, were intent on carrying on the work of denting, if not destroying, the Australian monopoly. Meanwhile, in Australia, the leaders of the LTA placed implicit trust in the ability of Harry Hopman to continue master-minding the Down Under players, despite Laver's defection and Fraser's determination to retire. Roy Emerson was now looked upon as the heir-apparent to Laver's crown and his ambition was furthered when he became an employee of Philip Morris Inc. (Australian division), a company with a tennis fan and a philanthropist for president.

With no Laver or Fraser to block his path, Roy Emerson was the best in the world. His road to the Australian title was a comparatively easy one, with only Bob Hewitt, Ken Fletcher and Fred Stolle at home to bar his way. He immediately set forth on his world travels, arriving at New York in time to enter the U. S. Indoor Championships where he was defeated in the quarter-final by Eugene Scott. When Dennis Ralston beat McKinley in the final, the composition of the American Davis Cup team was assured.

As the entry for the Davis Cup increased to 32 nations in the European Zone, a preliminary round was necessary. The seeded nations – Sweden, South Africa, Great Britain and Italy – did not enter the lists until the second round. The eight survivors for the quarter-finals were Sweden, Yugoslavia, South Africa, Denmark, Russia, Great Britain, France and Spain. There were nine entries in the Eastern Zone and seven in the American, bringing the total challengers to forty-eight, the largest entry in several years.

Manuel Santana had the best record on the Florida-Caribbean tour but when the Riviera season got into full swing, the South Africans, Yugoslavs and Italians made their presence felt. Marty Mulligan of Australia won the Italian title after Boro Jovanovic upset Emerson. Pierre Darmon beat

Rod Laver. (Courtesy *World Tennis)*

Santana at Paris but gave Emerson his second leg on the Grand Slam. The Wimbledon quarter-finalists were Emerson and Stolle of Australia, McKinley and Frank Froehling of United States, Wilhelm Bungert and Christian Kuhnke of Germany, Bobby Wilson of Great Britain and Manuel Santana of Spain. Bungert upset Emerson and Stolle beat Santana to reach the semi-finals. In the final McKinley defeated Stolle in straight sets.

While the Australians continued their tour of the Continental tournaments, Great Britain defeated Spain 4-1 at Bristol while Sweden defeated South Africa at Bastaad to become the European Zone finalists. India and Japan were finalists in Asia and India defeated Japan 3-2 to win the Eastern Zone. The United States beat Iran in Teheran and then overcame their most serious obstacle by beating Rafe Osuna and Antonio Palafox 4-1 after McKinley had lost the opening match to Osuna. The doubles was the great surprise as McKinley and Ralston downed the Wimbledon and American doubles champions, Osuna-Palafox, in straight sets 6-1, 6-3, 8-6.

In the American Zone final, the United States defeated Venezuela 5-0; in Europe, Great Britain defeated Sweden 4-1. The rules of the draw now brought the United States and Great Britain together, with Britain having the choice of ground. It was the first time since 1936 that Britain had reached the Interzone final and they chose the hard court of Bournemouth as the battleground. Both teams surprised in their choice of players. Captain Duncan Macaulay named Billy Knight instead of Bobby Wilson as England's second singles player, while Captain Kelleher chose Frank Froehling instead of Ralston. In the American Championships, just completed, Froehling had reached the final, beating Emerson, Wilson and Barnes of Brazil before losing to Osuna. It was a walk-over for the Americans. McKinley beat Sangster 7-5, 6-2, 7-5, and Knight 8-6, 6-2, 6-3. Froehling downed Knight 4-6, 8-6, 6-4, 6-4 and Sangster 6-1, 4-6, 6-0, 6-4. McKinley-Ralston then conquered Wilson-Sangster 6-4, 6-8, 9-7, 6-2.

There was still one more bridge to be crossed and India was waiting on the way to the Challenge Round. Early in November on the rubble courts at Bombay, McKinley and Ralston beat Krishnan, Lall and Mukerjea by 5 rubbers to 0 and again became the Challengers after a lapse of three years.

Both captains had some difficulty in selecting their teams. Froehling, who had beaten both Englishmen in the first Interzone final, fell ill and Captain Kelleher had to rely on Ralston for both singles and doubles. Fraser, who had attempted a comeback, was chosen by Captain Hopman to play the doubles with Emerson. Stolle, who had had the best record among the other Australians in the State title events, was sidetracked in favor of a young player, John Newcombe. As later events proved, this was a poor gamble as Newcombe lost both his singles—to Ralston in the opening match 6-4, 6-1, 3-6, 4-6, 7-5 and to McKinley in the last one 10-12, 6-2, 9-7, 6-2. In the doubles Fraser was only a shadow of his former self, and even at his best Emerson was not able to carry him. So this crucial point went also to the challengers 6-3, 4-6, 11-9, 11-9, giving America the Cup by three rubbers to two.

Soon after the Cup was returned to America, amidst the usual celebrations, it began to appear that it was there for a long stay. The Australian LTA shut the gates on its ranking players by forbidding them to leave the homeland before the early spring. When Emerson and Fletcher and later Stolle refused to obey the ban of the officials, it appeared as though America might once again obtain a long tenure of the Cup. The leading Australian players who defied their officials were formally banned from representing their country by the Australian LTA. At the USLTA Annual Meeting, the venue of the Challenge Round was set for Cleveland and, for the first time in America, on a surface other than grass.

Emerson, Fletcher, Osuna, and Palafox turned up in Salisbury, Maryland, for the U. S. Indoors. Emerson was beaten in the second round and Santana in the quarter-finals. From there Emerson and Fletcher competed in the Florida-Caribbean Circuit where Emmo had two losses—to Ron Holmberg and Froehling. But as soon as his feet touched European soil, he became unbeatable—until he reached Paris where he lost in the quarter-finals to Pietrangeli in straight sets. Ralston remained in America until he had won the National Intercollegiate title for the second time. Then he hastened to Wimbledon where he was joined by McKinley, winner of the Bristol event, and other American players.

One of the surprises of the early round Davis Cup ties was Spain's defeat by Denmark when Juan Manuel Couder lost both his singles and Santana-Lis Arilla were defeated by Jan Leschly-Jorgen Ulrich. Just before Wimbledon, in the semi-finals, Great Britain defeated Yugoslavia at Manchester 3-2 while Germany beat Denmark at Munich 4-1. Sweden accounted for Italy at Turin 3-1, Pietrangeli's win over Ulf Schmidt being the Italians' only point. France had a close match against South Africa at Paris, being 2-0 down at the end of the first day. In the European Zone final, Sweden beat France at Bastaad 4-1 and qualified for the Interzones.

At Wimbledon Emerson took up where he had left off and went through like a whirlwind. McKinley reached the semi-finals where he lost to Stolle in four sets, but Ralston who had flown in after winning the Intercollegiate title was upset in his first match by Tony Pickard of Britain.

The cheers had hardly died down after Emerson's win over Stolle in the

Wimbledon final when the cables began to hum. Norman Strange, head of the Australian LTA who had been so adamant in February, softened like a sponge in July. Just a little tiny "Sorry, sir" and Emerson and Stolle were hastily reinstated and Newcombe, Fletcher and the others who were to fight in a lost cause were shelved. The challenging team, with Harry Hopman in charge, was reconstituted and hurried off to Mexico after an easy match over Canada. The American Association, which had anticipated a Challenge Round with Mexico its opponent and had set the locale at Cleveland on a composition court, were chagrined but could do nothing about it. Although the Australian team played in the U.S. Championships on grass with Emerson the winner and Stolle the runner-up, they were tempted by an offer of $50,000 to play the Interzone final against Sweden at Bastaad on clay rather than in America on grass. It gave the Swedes a far better chance. Nevertheless Australia won despite a crucial 5-2 in the fifth set lead by Lundquist over Emerson.

The Challenge Round was played on a specially constructed composition court in a park in Cleveland, Ohio, from September 25 to 28. A fourth day's play was made necessary by the weather conditions on the Sunday which delayed the fourth match to such a late hour that the fifth and final rubber could not be commenced and was postponed to Monday. The Australians were slightly favored, but the Americans put up a courageous battle. McKinley met Stolle in the first match and defeated him 6-1, 9-7, 4-6, 6-2. In the second match Emerson defeated Ralston quite easily 6-3, 6-1, 6-2. This was the anticipated result and when the Americans pulled out a close doubles after being down two sets to one, 6-4, 4-6, 4-6, 6-3, 6-4, hopes ran high.

At Forest Hills three weeks previously Stolle had beaten Ralston in a match interrupted by an overnight wait with the score at two sets all. Here again at Cleveland weather played its part so that Ralston, after being two sets behind, pulled out the third and fourth only to lose the decider (after having an early service break) at 6-4 to bring the score to two rubbers each. Though McKinley did everything he could be bring Emerson down, it was a lost cause and, once more, after a sojourn of less than a year, the Davis Cup returned to Australia with the score between the two countries now tied again at nineteen victories apiece.

22

New Challenge-Same Result

Hardly had the victorious team returned with the Davis Cup to Australia than the Americans suffered two grievous losses. Jim Dickey, the president of the USLTA, fell ill and died in Fort Lauderdale, Florida, on October 19, 1964. He was seventy-two years old. Dickey had been identified with tennis for many years. He had been president of the Eastern LTA, one of the largest sections in the USLTA, for several years before moving to Florida. In the controversy over open tennis he had taken a neutral stand and his entire career had been marked by moderation in the bitter struggles among his associates on the Executive Committee of the USLTA.

At almost the same time that Dickey passed away, Chuck McKinley let it be known that he was no longer available for the U. S. Davis Cup team. He had now graduated from college and had taken a position with a New York investment firm where he intended to devote himself to a business career.

Dickey's successor as president of the USLTA was Martin Tressel of Pittsburgh, Pa. Tressel had been nominated as second vice-president in 1962 and advanced to first vice-president when Dickey assumed the presidency in 1964. Tressel was an avowed opponent of open tennis and, behind the scenes, led the group which brought about the approval by the USLTA of a resolution opposing open tournaments and committing the USLTA to continue defeatism whenever the question might be raised in the International Federation.

It had been the custom for some time for the incoming president of the USLTA when there was a change of officers to give an interview or write an article outlining his plans for his administration. When Tressel was asked, shortly after Dickey's funeral, to continue this custom, he declined, giving as his reasons that he was not yet president *de facto* and furthermore, when he was, by election at the forthcoming Annual Meeting in February, he would first consult with Perry Jones, the powerful head of the

Southern California Section. One result of this conference was the appointment as Davis Cup captain of a Southern Californian, George MacCall, a senior as a player and sometime partner of Bob Kelleher, the previous Davis Cup captain. Most of the USLTA brass acclaimed MacCall's appointment though some adopted a "let's wait and see" attitude.

When the draw for the 1965 contest was announced by Australia, the champion nation, it was found to comprise 31 nations in the European Zone, 9 in the Eastern Zone, and 5 in the American Zone, a total of 45. As usual the eight quarter-finalists of 1964 were seeded in the European Zone and thus, with France which drew a bye, won their way without trouble into the second round. Italy beat Portugal, Germany beat Switzerland, Spain beat Greece, South Africa beat the Netherlands and Yugoslavia beat Morocco, all by 5-0 scores. Sweden lost one match to Poland and Great Britain lost to Israel. Of the unseeded nations, Czechoslovakia had a default from Monaco, Norway one from the United Arab Republic, and Rhodesia one from Russia. Austria lost one match to Finland and Chile one to Belgium. Brazil and Luxemburg had 3-2 wins over Hungary and Turkey, while Denmark had a 3-0 win over Ireland.

In the Eastern Zone, Korea, Malaysia and Ceylon drew byes; Japan won over the Philippines and India over Iran by 5-0 scores and Vietnam defeated Pakistan 4-1. In the American Zone, New Zealand beat British Caribbean 5-0 while United States, Mexico and Canada drew byes.

During April, the contest in the Eastern Zone reached the final between the two sections. In Section A, the Japanese team of Osamo Ishiguro, Ichize Konishi and Koji Watanabe beat the Philippines and then South Korea, both by 5-0 scores, to qualify against India. With Krishnan, India's leading player, in America for the Caribbean circuit, Mukerjea and Lall won for India over Iran, Ceylon and Vietnam to qualify for the Asian semi-final. In the American Zone Mexico beat New Zealand 5-0 while United States, represented by Gene Scott, Arthur Ashe, Chuck McKinley and Martin Riessen, beat Canada 5-0. Ralston, the United States' number one player, was not included in the American team as he had been suspended by Captain MacCall even though the tie against Canada was to be played in Bakersfield, California, Ralston's home town. MacCall said, "Ralston walked out on Richardson (his doubles partner) and went home after losing to him in the singles."

The second round in Europe was played during the week ending May 16. Germany beat Luxembourg, Spain beat Chile, South Africa beat Norway, Yugoslavia beat Rhodesia and France beat Austria, all by 5-0 scores while Great Britain beat Denmark 3-1. Italy had a close match with Brazil. Pietrangeli beat both Barnes and Koch in straight sets and Merlo also won in straight sets over Koch. However, the Brazilians won the doubles and Barnes beat Merlo to make the final score 3-2. The big surprise was the Czechs' defeat of the favored Swedes. Lundquist won both his singles from Holocek and Javorsky but the second Swede, Olander, not only lost both of his singles but, paired with Lundquist, lost the doubles in four sets to Javorsky-Koudelka.

During the week of June 13, between the French championships and Wimbledon, the quarter-finals of the European Zone were played. Czechoslovakia, with Holocek and Javorsky, defeated the favored Italian team of Pietrangeli, Merlo and Tacchini 3-2 with Pietrangeli alone accounting for the two Italian wins. France, with Darmon, Barthes and Jauffret, beat the Yugoslavs, Pilic and Jovanovic, at Paris 5-0 while Spain, with Santana, Gisbert and Arilla, won over Bungert, Buding and Kuhnke of Germany 4-1, Gisbert losing to Buding for the only German win. The big upset of the round was South Africa's win over Great Britain at Eastbourne by three rubbers to two. On the first day Sangster lost to Diepraam and Taylor to Drysdale. The British team of Sangster and Wilson won the doubles from Segal and Diepraam but Drysdale took the clinching point when he beat Sangster in four sets. There were now four teams left in Europe, two in Asia and two in America.

The European semi-finals were played during the weekend of July 18. At Paris South Africa beat France 4-1. Drysdale won both his matches from Barthes and Darmon and the doubles too. The only French point was won by Darmon on the first day when he beat Diepraam in five sets. On the same weekend Spain beat the Czech team with only one loss, when Javorsky beat Juan Gisbert. Santana won both his matches and Santana–Arilla won the doubles 6-2, 6-2, 6-3. The final was another 4-1 win for Spain at Barcelona on the August 1 weekend, the only Spanish loss being once more Gisbert's loss to Drysdale in four sets.

In the American Zone final Mexico had choice of ground but was persuaded for financial reasons to play in Dallas. Ashe and Ralston played the singles and Ralston-Richardson the doubles for United States while the tried and true Mexican pair of Osuna–Palafox carried the Mexican banner. The only Mexican win was the doubles, 8-6, 6-4, 7-5.

The final of the Asian Zone was played in Tokyo the first week in October and Krishnan-Mukerjea played both singles and doubles for India while Watanabe-Ishigura represented Japan. The doubles was the only Japanese victory.

Captain MacCall had a big decision to make when he took his team, the American Zone winners, to Barcelona for the Interzone final against Spain. Ralston was sure for the Number One singles but would it be Ashe or Froehling for Number Two? Ashe had played magnificently against the

Mexicans in Dallas but Froehling was thought by MacCall and by Gonzales, the coach, to be better than Ashe on the rubble at Barcelona. It was conceded that Santana would win one and possibly two singles but it was hoped that Froehling and Ralston would both beat Gisbert and that America would win the doubles. However, when Ralston met Gisbert in the first match, he won the first set 6-3 and lost the second in a cliff-hanger at 10-8, then went all to pieces and lost the next two 6-1, 6-3. Froehling played his best against Santana but it was no contest. The score was 6-1, 6-4, 6-4 and Spain was two-up. Graebner was named with Ralston for the doubles against Santana-Arilla who had not lost a doubles in five rounds of Davis Cup play. The Americans got off to a good start and took the first two sets 6-4, 6-3. Spain tied it up by winning the third and fourth 6-3, 6-4 and the Americans were only two points away when they led in the fifth set 5-2 and 5-3. But Santana's backhand passing shot put the Spaniards at advantage in the 19th game. Then Graebner unsighted an overhead and Arilla held service for set and match. The crowd went wild.

The Eastern Zone winner, India, came to Barcelona to meet Spain in the Interzone final. Gisbert lost both his matches to Krishnan and Mukerjea but it made no difference. Santana won both his and the unbeaten Spanish doubles team made the score 3-2. Spain was in the Challenge Round for the first time.

The tie was played at Sydney on December 27 and 28 and at the end of the second day the champion nation had accounted for its 20th victory.

The surprise started on the first day in the first match when the Spanish hero, Manolo Santana, was beaten by Fred Stolle after winning the first two sets, 12-10, 6-3. At this stage Santana looked like an almost certain winner. But Stolle came back in the third like a whirlwind, broke Santana's service twice for a 5-4 lead, and held his own to take the fourth set and tie the score at two sets apiece. However, Santana was not yet beaten and came back strongly in the fifth set to carry the score to 5-all. Stolle held on and won the match in the twelfth game.

The second match was hardly more than a formality, for Emerson beat Gisbert easily, 6-3, 6-2, 6-2. In the doubles on the second day, Newcombe-Roche defeated Santana-Arilla 6-3, 4-6, 7-5, 6-2 to complete the defense of the Cup. On the third day, with nothing at stake, Santana justified his Number One ranking in the World by beating Emerson in four sets 2-6, 6-3, 6-4, 15-13 and Stolle took care of Gisbert 6-2, 6-4, 8-6.

When the Davis Cup nations met at London in July, 1965, the most important subject on the agenda was the report of the Special Committee which had been appointed to seek ways of curing the congestion of nations in the European Zone. For some years there had been no bar against an Eastern or American naion challenging in another zone. This led inevitably to a decline in nations challenging in other than the European Zone and causing a difficult problem in Europe. The solution presented to and approved by the delegates was merely a suggestion to be tried out in 1966. There was no problem in either the Eastern or American zone and six nations entered in the American Zone. Argentina and Chile were drawn in the first round, the winner to meet Mexico in the second, while Jamaica and Venezuela also met in the first round, the winner to meet the United States in the second. Seven nations were drawn in the Eastern Zone. Ceylon, Malasia, Philippines, South Korea, India and Iran were drawn in the first round with Japan a bye. The European Zone was divided into two sections, each with sixteen entries. The winner of Zone A was to meet the winner of the American Zone; while the winner of Zone B was to meet the winner of the Eastern Zone, the two zone winners to meet in an Interzone final to produce the challenger of Australia, the champion nation.

The first ties in the Eastern Zone were held in March and April with India the winner over Iran 5-0, Philippines over South Korea 3-2 and Ceylon over Malaysia 4-1. In the semi-finals, held the second week in May, India beat Ceylon 5-0 and Japan beat Philippines 3-2. The final between India and Japan was not held until October when the Indian team of Krishnan-Lall beat Ishigura-Watanabe of Japan 4-1, Watanabe's win over Lall being the only Japanese victory.

In the American Zone, Argentina beat Chile and Jamaica beat Venezuela in the first round, both 3-2. The United States and Mexico drew byes and in May the United States beat Jamaica 4-1 while Mexico beat Argentina by the same score. Ashe and Richey played singles for the United States with Pasarell teaming with Ashe in the doubles. The final between Mexico and the United States was set for mid-August in Cleveland, Ohio. The United States team of Ralston, Graebner and Richey defeated the Mexican team of Osuna, Loyo-Mayo and Lara by 3 matches to none.

In the European Zone A, with Spain, Sweden, France and Czechoslovakia seeded the only surprise was Poland's 3-2 win over Sweden. In Zone B with West Germany, Great Britain, Italy and South Africa seeded, there were no surprises. The second round was played the first weekend of May and in Zone A Poland beat Egypt 4-1, France beat Canada 5-0 and Czechoslovakia beat Israel by the same score. The big surprise was when Spain, last year's challenger, lost to Brazil 3-2. Ronnie Barnes had been suspended by the Brazilian Association because of some ill-timed remarks about his earnings from tennis. Koch and Mandarino were the Brazilian players. Gisbert beat Koch and Santana beat Mandarino on the first day to put Spain ahead but on the second day the Brazilian doubles team upset the Spaniards in five sets. On the third day Koch pulled a stunning surprise by beating Santana in straight sets, 7-5, 6-2, 6-1 to tie the score and an inspired Mandarino took the deciding point by outlasting Gisbert in a thriller 7-5, 3-6, 9-11, 8-6, 8-6. In Zone B there were no surprises. Germany beat Switzerland, Great Britain beat Hungary, Italy beat Morocco and South Africa beat Holland.

The semi-finals were played the weekend of June 12. In the upper half Brazil beat Poland and France beat Czechoslovakia, each by a 4-1 score. The results in Zone B were closer and more unexpected. At Hanover the German team of Buding and Bungert beat the British team of Sangster, Taylor and Wilson 3-2. The Germans led 2-0 on the first day, dropped the doubles after losing the first set 6-0 and lost another point when Taylor beat Buding as the German defaulted at one-all in the fourth set. South Africa also had a close 3-2 win over Italy at Rome. The Italians won the opening singles when Tacchini beat Drysdale and Pietrangeli beat Diepraam. The Italians also led two sets to love in the doubles but McMillan-Diepraam pulled it out by taking the next three. Then Drysdale beat Pietrangeli in five sets and Diepraam beat Tacchini in three to reach the Zone B final.

The finals in both Zones were played after Wimbledon the weekend of July 18. In Zone A Brazil completed its triumph with a 4-1 win over France, Darmon's defeat of Koch on the third day being the only French victory. Germany had a tougher win over South Africa in Zone B at Munich. The Germans got away to a 2-0 lead on the first day when Bungert beat Drysdale and Buding beat Diepraam, both in four sets. The doubles went to the South Africans, but Bungert beat Diepraam in straight sets to win the tie. Buding lost to Drysdale in the fifth match at 6-0 in the fourth set. The Interzones were now set, Brazil to meet United States and India to meet West Germany. The results of both ties were quite unexpected and that of the Interzone final even more so. The Davis Cup thus became not only an international but an Intercontinental prize.

The leaders of the United States Lawn Tennis Association, having suffered six years were determined to leave nothing undone in 1966 to restore their *amour propre.* Their Captain MacCall, a clever player in his own right, was given plenary powers by President Tressel. In a dictatorial manner which was in no way justified by the end results, he first lost the good will of the Richey family by insisting on a training regime including diet which was not approved by Richey's father and coach. Then he suspended the number one player, Ralston, for defaulting in a Texas tournament but promptly restored both these boys to good standing when he needed them. In order to concentrate control in his own hands he bent, if not broke, the time-hallowed interpretation of the amateur rules by announcing that he was going to pay regular salaries to the members of his self-appointed Cup team thus arousing the question if this was not, in effect if not in fact, a violation of the amateur regulations of the ILTF and the principles of amateurism which his superior, Tressel, had used as a stepping stone in his rise to the presidency of the USLTA.

Now, just on the verge of the next-to-last step on the road to the Challenge Round, MacCall and Tressel did everything possible to have the match with Brazil played in the United States. But Brazil quite properly refused to be a doormat and appealed to the champion nation, Australia, whose president refused to intervene. So the site of the tie was placed in Porto Alegre, Brazil, for the weekend of November 9. The result was a stunning blow, for the Brazilian team won the tie, three rubbers to two.

Captain MacCall repeated his mistake of 1965 in naming his team. Instead of picking Ashe for his second singles entry he named Richey, as he had chosen Froehling in 1965 and on the same grounds, that Ashe was not as good a clay court player. Richey, it is true, had just won a local tournament but on the first day, after Ralston had beaten Koch 6-4, 6-4, 6-0 in the opening match, Richey lost to Mandarino after taking the first set 7-5. Ashe teamed with Ralston to win the doubles as expected 7-5, 6-4, 4-6, 6-2 and things looked bright even after Richey fell to Koch 6-1, 7-5, 6-1. Mandarino whose courage, if not always his skill, had carried his team thus far was not to be denied and, in the deciding match, after being down one set to two, made a magnificent comeback and took the last two sets and the tie 6-4, 6-1. Neither Ralston nor MacCall have been able to explain convincingly how this happened.

After this the rest seemed anticlimatic. With Krishnan leading the way, India defeated Weat Germany 3-2. Krishnan beat Bungert in the opening match 7-5, 7-5, 6-4 and Mukerjea beat Buding 2-6, 7-5, 6-3, 6-4. The Germans defeated Lal-Mukerjea to take the doubles 6-1, 10-8, 6-4 but Mukerjea won the needed point when he beat Bungert 4-6, 8-6, 8-6, 6-3. Buding's win over Lall in five sets gave Germany a second point.

The Brazilians now came to Calcutta where they met the Indians on grass. The first day's matches were split when Koch beat Mukerjea 6-2, 6-2, 6-3. Krishnan tied it up when he defeated Mandarino 5-7, 6-2, 6-3, 6-2. India's hopes were high when they won a close doubles 7-5, 3-6, 6-3, 3-6, 6-3 but Brazil tied it up when Mandarino played his role of savior by defeating Mukerjea 9-7, 3-6, 8-6, 3-6, 7-5. Krishnan battled back from the brink of defeat to beat Koch 3-6, 6-4, 10-12, 7-5, 6-2. India was in the Challenge Round for the first time. Hope fell for India when the match was postponed the previous day with Brazil leading in the fourth set 5-2. But Krishnan broke Koch's service to level the match at two sets all. After Krishnan got his third straight service break in the fifth set, Koch's resistance collapsed. Krishnan got a 4-0 lead, dropped the next two games and finally clinched the set, the match and the tie 6-2.

It would have been a matter of great historic importance if India had only followed up this surprising feat of reaching the Challenge Round by defeating the Champion Nation in the final encounter, played at Melbourne on December 27-29, before 11,000 spectators. It was the first time India–in fact any Asian nation except Japan in the long distant past–had come so far. The draw brought Krishnan against Stolle in the opening match. "Krish's" touch game was of no value against sheer power and Stolle won the match in 74 minutes 6-3, 6-2, 6-4.

Mukerjea played a much more aggressive game against Emerson but was only in the match for fifteen minutes when he carried Emmo to 7-5 in the first set. The next two sets went to Emerson 6-4, 6-2.

With Australia two rubbers up and their 1965 champions, Newcombe and Roche, taking the court for the doubles, few expected the tie to go any farther. But the Indians did win and it was bit of a fluke. The hero of the match was Mukerjea in the first set and Krishnan in the second. The Indians won in four sets 4-6, 7-5, 6-4, 6-4. On the last day Emerson beat Krishnan 6-0, 6-2, 10-8 to retain the Cup for another year. In the last, meaningless match, Stolle beat Mukerjea in five sets, 7-5, 6-8, 6-3, 5-7, 6-3.

23

Will This Be the End?

When the Davis Cup nations met in London in July, 1966, the year's contest had barely got under way. Yet it was apparent, even that early, that further tinkering with the draw was called for. The full complement of thirty-two nations had entered in the already overcrowded European Zone which had therefore been divided into Zones A and B of sixteen nations each with the eight "seeds" which would have been held out of the first round divided, four apiece, into each Zone. Yet, among the indisputably European nations, there were Turkey, Canada, Brazil, Israel, South Africa, Chile, and the United Arab Republic. Besides these "European" nations, there were seven in the American Zone, three in South America – Argentina, Venezuela and Ecuador – plus a complete outsider, New Zealand, who elected to enter. There was also the Eastern Zone with eight entries, making a total of 47 nations in all. The draw also provided that the American Zone winner would meet the European Zone "A" champion in one semi-final while the European Zone "B" winner would meet the Eastern Zone champion in the other. Finally, the two Interzone winners would play each other for the right to battle the champion nation – Australia – in the Challenge Round.

The first tie in the Eastern Zone was held in Manila, March 25-27 when the Philippine stalwarts of many years standing, Raymundo Deyro and Felicisimo Ampon, beat the South Korean team of Kim Doo Huan and Chuch Yang Im 5-0, allowing their opponents no sets and only twelve games in the two singles matches. Their substitutes, Sammy Ang and Eduardo Cruz, did about as well in the doubles and the two final singles. On the weekend of April 8-10 two other ties in the Eastern Zone were played. Philippines beat South Vietnam at Manila 5-0. Only Ampon took the court for his side, winning his match 6-4, 6-1, 6-1. At Jakarta, Japan had a 5-0 walkover against Indonesia.

In the first ties in the American Zone, Mexico beat New Zealand at Mexico City on April 15, 16 and 17 by four rubbers to one. The only

New Zealand win was that of Brian Fairlie over Rafe Osuna 6-4, 2-6, 6-3, 4-6, 6-3. The other New Zealand players were not in Fairlie's class and lost both the second singles to Marcelo Lara as well as the doubles. In another American Zone tie played at Trinidad the weekend of April 30, the United States team of Pasarell and Richey for the singles with Graebner-Riessen for the doubles defeated the British West Indies team of Lumsden and Russell 5-0 with the loss of only one set.

First round matches in the European Zone commenced on the weekend of April 30 and continued on the weekend of May 7. Of the sixteen ties six were won 5-0 and three more by scores of 4-1, leaving only six to go the limit. Luxembourg beat Ireland, Greece beat Switzerland, Brazil beat Yugoslavia, South Africa beat Netherlands, Russia beat Germany, and Chile beat Czechoslovakia, all by 4-3 scores. The matches which caused the most surprise were Tom Okker's and Jan Hajer's wins over Cliff Drysdale. Bob Hewitt, playing for South Africa for the first time, not only won both his singles, but teamed with Frew MacMillan for a straight set victory in the doubles. Chile's win over the Czechs at Prague came down to the last match when Patrice Rodriguez defeated the Czech ace, Milan Holocek, at 7-5 in the fifth set. The big surprise was Russia's win over last year's zone champions, Germany, at Dusseldorf. At the end of the first day the teams were tied with Metreveli's win over Buding and Bungert's win over Lejus. Likhachev-Metreveli teamed to defeat Bungert-Buding in four hard-fought sets. Buding defeated Lejus to even the score but Bungert was unable to carry the day for the Germans when he unaccountably lost to Metreveli at 7-5 in the fifth set after having a two sets to one lead. Mike Belkin was on the way to becoming Canada's hero when he defeated Mike Sangster in four sets in the opening singles. But Bob Bedard, who had been through many a Cup match, proved to be an easy victim for both Taylor and Sangster. Another former finalist went down to defeat when Gulyas won both his singles against Lundquist and Bengsten and masterminded the doubles as well. Lundquist's defeat of Szikszai was the only Swedish victory.

Of the eight ties in the second round, played during the weekend of May 21, five were won by 5-0 scores. France, with two youngsters, Goven and Jauffret, whitewashed Hungary at Paris; Mandarino and Koch of Brazil defeated Poland at Warsaw; South Africa with Drysdale, Hewitt and MacMillan conquered Monaco at Monte Carlo; England beat Bulgaria at Sofia and Italy beat Luxembourg at Piacenza. Russia had to go to the fifth match when Metreveli beat Torben Ulrich to defeat Denmark; Spain had to rely on Santana to defeat Tiriac of Roumania; and Chile won over Greece when Rodriguez came from two sets to love down to upset

Gavrilidis. In the American Zone, United States and Ecuador reached the final. Ecuador beat Argentina at Buenos Aires and the United States defeated Mexico in Mexico City, the score in both matches being 4-1. For Mexico, Osuna won the only point when he defeated Richey; Ashe beat both Osuna and Lara in straight sets as did Graebner-Riessen over Osuna—Loyo-Mayo in the doubles. In the Eastern Zone India reached the final with a win over Iran, four matches to one.

The four quarter-final matches in the European Zone were played, as usual, between the French and Wimbledon championships. In Zone A, Spain beat Britain at Eastbourne 3-1 when Santana beat Sangster in a close match 8-10, 6-3, 5-7, 9-7, 6-0 while Taylor beat Arilla in four sets. The doubles went to the Spaniards as expected in straight sets and Santana won the odd match over Taylor 6-4, 6-3, 7-5. To qualify for the semi-final in Zone B Russia beat Chile 3-0. Metreveli defeated Pinto-Bravo in four sets, Lejus beat Rodriguez, also in four, and Metreveli-Likhajev won the doubles over Pinto-Bravo—Cornejo 7-5, 6-1, 6-2. The other two ties were cancelled because of rain. Russia's opponent for the final proved to be South Africa who defeated France 5-0, losing only two sets. Jauffret won one from Hewitt and Beust-Contet won the other from Hewitt-MacMillan.

During the customary hiatus in Europe during the Italian and French championships, the American Zone final between Ecuador and United States was played at Guyaquil on June 17, 18 and 19. It was the surprise of the year and the most shocking defeat of an American Davis Cup team since the Italians, Pietrangeli and Sirola, pulled up from 0-2 down against Dave Freed's team of MacKay, Buchholz and McKinley in 1960.

There was no hassle about the venue of the tie as there had been the year before. George MacCall had been appointed Davis Cup captain by Bob Kelleher, a fellow Californian and a former Davis Cup captain (the last one to lead a challenging team to victory). It appeared to some that Kelleher had acted rather hastily, perhaps in response to MacCall's plea to give him one more chance. At any rate, the Interzone tie with Mexico in which Ashe distinguished himself justified MacCall's action in selecting Ashe and Richey (the presumed clay court specialist) for the singles and who but the well-seasoned pair of Marty Riessen and Clark Graebner for the doubles. At least, some argued, there would be no risk of a final match fall-down by the new professional, Dennis Ralston.

So, instead of taking along Coach Pancho Gonzales for intensive practice, at a sizeable fee, MacCall simply allowed ten days of practice on the clay courts to permit the Americans to become accustomed to the surface. As Guzman, the son of a Guayaquil banker who was not considered to be the equal of his teammate Miguel Olvera, was drawn against Richey, a two-love margin at the end of the first day was looked for. Richey opened the match aggressively and won the first set handily at 6-2. But Guzman won the second set by the same score to even the match. Though the Ecuadorian fought hard Richey had too much experience and pulled out the third set 8-6 and then won the fourth for the first American point at 6-4.

When Olvera and Ashe stepped on the court for the second match no trouble was looked for. MacCall had been criticized for not using Ashe in the matches against Spain and Brazil in his two previous terms as Davis Cup captain. He was determined not to make the same mistake in his third try – and for his fellow Californian, Kelleher, whose confidence in him had been severely criticized in some quarters. But, if he expected Ashe to redeem the previous mistakes, he must have been highly disappointed by Olvera, the son of a poor family and a former ball-boy whose promising career of a few years back had been cut short by a siege of tuberculosis and had only recently returned to competition.

Ashe, full of confidence, started off well, winning the first four points on his big service. He went on to win the first set 6-4 but Olvera, standing up well to Ashe's service and playing mostly from the back court, won both the second and third sets by the same score. At this point play was halted because of darkness. As Olvera had to play the doubles next day, a strong comeback by Ashe was looked for. But Olvera went ahead early and won the set 6-2 and the match to even the tie.

None of the Americans worried in the least when Graebner and Riessen took the court in the afternoon against a tired Olvera and an aggressive Guzman. Playing every stroke to Guzman who was felt to be the weak man on the team, the Americans quickly went ahead, running off the first set 6-0 and getting a 1-0 lead in the second. But Guzman came to life in the second set and, with admirable help from Olvera, they won both the second and third sets 9-7, 6-3. The Americans reacted after the intermission and won the fourth set 6-4 to even the match but though they several times had a point for the break in the fifth set, they could not win any of them. The set went to Ecuador at 8-6 and now they had a 2-1 lead.

The stadium was filled to capacity as the Ecuadorian crowd smelled the sweet scent of victory. But Captain MacCall had no worry as Arthur Ashe went off to a lead by winning the first set at love. But he soon showed that he did not have what it takes when his game fell off as Guzman's improved. The Ecuadorian went ahead by winning the second and third sets 6-4, 6-2 but was very tired at the intermission and, when play was resumed, Ashe took another love set to even the match. In the fifth set Ashe was serving hard and going to the net at every opportunity. But Guzman was determined not to let down, broke Ashe's service in the first game but was broken right back. Ashe had a chance for 3-1 when he led 30-40 on Guzman's service. It was now Ashe's turn to tire, whether for lack of practice or his Army service. Guzman, meanwhile, was improving with every point, went ahead and won the decisive match at 6-3 in the fifth set.

As often happens, the best match was played after the tie had been decided. Richey and Olvera were even at two sets all when an incident occurred which disturbed Olvera who gave away the meaningless set at love. For the third year in a row under MacCall's captaincy, the United States had been shut out of a trip to Australia and possible regeneration. It was a sad and discouraging experience.

The semi-finals in the European Zone were played following Wimbledon. At Barcelona, on July 16, Spain defeated Russia 4-1 Spain was two up on the first day as Santana beat Lejus 6-4, 6-4, 6-1 and Gisbert defeated Metreveli after losing the first two sets. However, the Russian doubles team of Metreveli-Likhachev kept the tie open when they defeated the strong and seasoned Spaniards, Santana-Arilla, on their home court 6-3, 3-6, 6-4, 6-4. Spain won the tie when Santana beat Metreveli 6-0, 6-3, 6-3 and Gisbert won another point by beating Lejus in four sets.

Neither of the finalists in Zone B was a European nation and as Brazil had held the Interzone final in 1966, the Zone final this year was awarded to South Africa. It was not really a close contest though some of the scores were less than overwhelming. The home team won all five ties, with Hewitt defeating Koch 6-4, 9-11, 11-9, 6-2 and Mandarino 1-6, 3-6, 6-4, 6-2, 6-0; Drysdale defeated Mandarino 6-2, 8-6, 6-2 and Koch 6-3, 8-6, 6-4; and Hewitt-MacMillan defeated the Brazilians 1-6, 4-6, 6-3, 6-4, 6-3.

The Interzone finals brought together Spain and Ecuador at Barcelona September 23 with a 5-0 victory for the Spanish team of Santana, Gisbert and Arilla. The doubles went to five sets with the South Americans leading two sets to one at the interval. Guzman also carried Gisbert to five sets so the South Americans were by no means disgraced.

The following week India once again won the Eastern Zone final with another victory over its arch-rival Japan, 4-1. Krishnan played only in the doubles and the Japanese point was won when Watanabe defeated Mukerjea in four sets. India than proceeded to Barcelona to meet defeat at the hands of South Africa in another semi-final Interzone tie 5-0. Both Hewitt and Drysdale beat the Indian No. 1, Krishnan, Hewitt 3-6, 6-3, 6-2, 2-6, 8-6, and Drysdale 7-5, 6-4, 3-6, 6-3.

U. S. champion Santana (left) of Spain, and Australian Roy Emerson. Emerson was champion in 1964, Santana in 1965. (Courtesy *World Tennis)*

Spain journeyed to South Africa for the Interzone final on December 4. Bob Hewitt, the South African No. 1 had been injured and Captain Claude Lister and Coach Jaroslav Drobny were put in an unfortunate quandary when the former Australian could not play. Ray Moore was chosen to play the second singles and Drysdale took Hewitt's place in the doubles. The Spaniards named young Manuel Ornates instead of Gisbert and the youngster proved that the future lay all before him, losing both to Drysdale and Moore though he carried Moore to five sets. It was not enough, however, for Santana won both his matches as well as the doubles with Arilla.

Once again the Spaniards journeyed to Australia for another try to bring home the Davis Cup. However the best they could do was to win one point when the incomparable Santana beat the Wimbledon champion, John Newcombe, in straight sets after the tie had already been won. The match was played at Brisbane before a slim attendance of only 7,000 on the first day when Spain had at least a fighting chance, and only 3,000 on the other two days when it was foregone that Australia had kept the Cup.

Captain Hopman decided to play Emerson instead of Roche in the singles alongside of the Wimbledon and American champion and his choice was well justified when Emmo defeated Santana handily 6-4, 6-1, 6-1. Newcombe followed with a straight set win over Orantes 6-3, 6-3, 6-2. The Spaniards suffered another mishap when Luis Arilla was injured in practice. Orantes substituted for him but Spanish teamwork which had survived so many tough spots in the past was hopeless before Newcombe and Roche. Santana won the sole Spanish point when he beat Newcombe on the third day 7-5, 6-4, 6-2, but Emmo taught Orantes a lesson by taking the final rubber 6-1, 6-2, 6-4.

24

Crisis

On October 5, 1967, the British Lawn Tennis Association took an historic step toward eliminating the hypocrisy of "shamateurism" which had plagued the tennis world for many years. The council voted 61 to 6 to end the distinction between amateurs and professionals and to call everyone "players." At its annual General Meeting on December 14, the decision of the council was overwhelmingly approved, to become effective April 22, at the start of the British Hard Court Championship at Bournemouth, the most important event on the calendar, next to Wimbledon.

The whole tennis world, both amateur and professional, was immediately aroused. The president of the International Lawn Tennis Federation, Giorgio di Stefani of Italy, in a tempestuous outburst, immediately wrote off the British Association as heretical and worse, though he actually had no authority to take such action. Meanwhile, the other leading nations, Australia, the United States and France, each, along with Britain, having twelve votes in the ILTF, began to ask themselves "What shall we do?" The lesser nations, too, began to debate their attitude. Sweden proposed an entirely new deal and a meeting of the ILTF to act on it. Germany withdrew from all international participation until the matter was clarified, Australia voted to support Britain, America took a temporizing attitude, France had a proposal of its own.

Although the Davis Cup competition is officially entitled The International Lawn Tennis Championship and has its own regulations, the contest is open to all members of the ILTF. One of the Davis Cup regulations provides that "any amateur who has never abandoned or lost his status as such shall be qualified to represent a nation . . . " This regulation, unless amended, would automatically disqualify any player who took part in an "open tournament" such as Wimbledon. Nevertheless, Australia, as holder of the Davis Cup, ignored the British action and acted as if nothing had happened. Despite the fact that 1968 might see the end

Sir Norman and Lady Brookes (left) welcome President and Mrs. Johnson to Australia. (Courtesy *World Tennis)*

of the competition, not only by adverse legislation but also because the amount of space left on the plaques surrounding the base of the Cup was getting limited to possibly no more than a single year, the draw for 1968 in the European Zone was made and promulgated with England, the rebel, drawn against France in the first round. Whether this match will ever take place, or, in fact, what the future of the Davis Cup itself may be, depends on the struggle which will be waged between the forces of honesty and hypocrisy which have fought each other since the first showdown in the International Federation in 1933.

At that time, the U. S. Lawn Tennis Association, endeavoring to keep its great champion, Tilden, under its dominion, offered a resolution at the ILTF meeting to permit so-called "open" tournaments. This was vigorously opposed by the European nations, headed by Chevalier de Borman of Belgium who said, "The day we open our gates to the professionals, all our point of view will change." Ever since that day, the "point of view" of the smaller nations has not changed an iota. It is still a matter of the coin of the realm or the "twenty pieces of silver" – the fear that by authorizing "Open Tennis" the goose that lays the golden eggs of Wimbledon, Forest Hills, Roland Garros, and even Melbourne, will be killed for the benefit of the "players" and at the expense of the officials of the so-called "Davis Cup Nations" who have lived off the fat of the land for more than half a century.

Apart from the question of honesty and "shamateurism" the Davis Cup, as a symbol of the universality of the game of "lawn tennis," has reached the end of its usefulness. With nearly fifty nations competing each year in teams of two to four players, the cost of travel and training is more and more becoming a drain on the treasuries of the smaller nations. When it is realized that after nearly seventy years of competition only four nations have been privileged to call themselves world champions, and that the expenses of a small nation, even though partly compensated by a subsidy from the so-called STE (Special Traveling Expense) Fund could probably be better used to improve the overall level of proficiency rather than sending just a few players on a world-wide junket, it seems that something better could be devised.

Much as those of us who have lived through these troubled years may hope that the Davis Cup, even if in name only, may continue to be the symbol of international friendship in the tennis world, is it traitorous at the same time to suggest that now, when the whole game of tennis stands at a crossroads, might be an opportune time to place the Davis Cup on a pedestal in the Hall of Fame and inaugurate a new era of international harmony and honesty during which the ideals of Dwight Davis are perpetuated as he saw them in his vision of 1900.

Roster of Players in the Davis Cup 1900 - 1968

I

YEARS	CHAPTERS	PAGES
1900-1907	1-3	9-25

Anderson, F.
Aymé, P.

Baddeley, W.
Barrett, H.R.
Beamish, Alfred
Behr, Karl
Black, E.D.
Brookes, Norman E.

Campbell, O.
Clarks, The
Clothier, W.J.
Collins, Kreigh
Collins, W.H.
Crescent Athletic Club

Dashiell, Paul
Davis, Dwight F.
De Borman, Paul
Decugis, Max

Doherty, Hugh L.
Doherty, Reginald F.
Dwight, Dr. James

Eames, C.G.
Eaves, Dr. W.V.

Freeman, L.

Germot, Paul
Goodbody, M.F.
Gore, A.W.
Hardys, The
Hillyard, George
Hobart, C.

LT The
Larned, W.A.
Lemaire, L.
Little, R.D.
Longwood C.C.

Mahony, H.S.
Meers, E.G.

Nisbet, H.

Pim, Dr. J.

Renshaw, W.
Riseley, F.

Sears, R.D.
Smith, Sydney

USNLTA

Ward, Holcombe
Whitman, M.D.
Wilding, A.F.
Wrenn, George
Wrenn, Robert D.
Wright, Beals C.

II

YEARS	CHAPTERS	PAGES
1908-1919	4-7	26-47

Alexander, Fred
Anderson, J.O.

Barrett, H. R.
Behr, Karl
Bemish, A.
Brookes, Norman
Browne, Mary
Bundy, Tom

Clothier, W.J.
Crawley, W.C.

Davson, P.
De Borman, Paul
Decugis, Max
Dixon, C.P.
Doust, S.
Dunlop, A.W.
Du Vicier, W.R.

Froitzheim, Otto

Garland, C.
Gauntlett, V.R.
Germot, P.
Gobert, André
Gore, A.W.

Hackett, H .
Heath, R.

I.L.T.F.

Johnston, W.M.
Jones, Arnold W.

Kingscote, A.
Kleinschroth, H.
Kreuzer, O.

Lammens, M.
Larned, W.A.
Laurentz, W.
Le Sueur, R.F.
Little, R.D.
Lowe, A.
Lowe, F.C.

Mavrogordato, T.M.
McLoughlin, Maurice
Murray, R.

Norton, B.I.C.

Parke, J.C.
Patterson, G.
Powell, R.E.

Rahe, F.
Raymond, L.
Rice, J.
Ritchie, M.J.G.

Schwengers, T.P.

Thomas, R.V.
Throckmorton, H.
Tilden, W.T. II

Watson, A.
W.S.T.C.
Wilding, A.
Wood, P O'H
Wright, B.C.

III

YEARS	CHAPTERS	PAGES
1920-1927	8-11	48-69

Aeschliman, C.
Alonso, M.
Ardelt, K.

Bennett, P.
Blanchy, P.
Borotra, J.
Brookes, N.
Brugnon, J.

Cochet, H.

Deane, L.
Decugis, Max
De Gomar, M.
Diemer Kool, A.

Feret, P.
Flaquer, E.
Fyzee, A.A.
Fyzee, A.H.

Garland, O.
Gilbert, J.
Gillou, P.
Gobert, A.
Godfree, L.
Gregory, J.

Harada, T.
Hardy, S.
Hawkes, J.
Heath, R.
Henriksen, P.
Hirsch, P.
Holmes, G.
Hunter, F.

Ingerslav, V.

Jacob, S.M.
Johnston, W.M.
Just, J.

Kehrling, B.
Kingscote, A.
Kinsey, H.
Kozeluh, J.
Kumagae, I.
Lacoste, R.
LaFramboise, H.
Landry, P.
Laurentz, W.
Lowe, F.G.
Lycett, R.

Macenauer, J.
Mavrogordato, T.
Mishu, N.
Morpurgo, U.
Muhr, A.

Norton, B.I.C.

Ohta, K.

Parke, J.
Patterson, G.
Peach, N.

Rasmussen, C.
Raymond, L.
Richards, V.
Riseley, F.

Samazeuilh, J.
Shimizu, Z.
Sleem, M.

Tarawa, I.
Tegner, E.
Tilden, W.T. 2nd
Toba, O.
Todd, C.
Turnbull, O.

Van Lennep, C.

Washburn, W.
Washer, J.
Watson, A.
Wertheim, R.
Williams, R.N.
Winslow, C.
Wood, P. O'H
Woosnam, M.

Zemla, L.

IV

YEARS	CHAPTERS	PAGES
1928-1950	12-17	70-100

Abdesselam, R.
Allison, W.
Austin, H.W.

Bergelin, L.
Bernard, M.
Borotra, J.
Boussus, C.
Brown, G.
Brown, T.
Brugnon, J.
Budge, J.D.

Cernik, V.
Cochet, H.
Cohn, J.
Collins, I.G.
Collum, S.
Cooke, E.

David, H.
Davidson, S.
Denker, H.
Destremau, B.
Di Stefani, G.
Dixon, F.
Doeg, J.
Drobny, J.

Falkenburg, R.
Farquharson, N.
Flam, H.
Froitzheim, O.

Gaslini, P.
Gledhill, K.
Gonzales, R.
Grant, B.

Harada, T.
Hare, C.
Harris, C.
Hecht, L.
Henkel, H.
Hennessey, J.
Herrick, M.
Hopman, H.
Hughes, G.
Hunt, G.
Hunt, J.
Hunter, F.

Johanssen, T.
Johnston, W.M.
Jones, Arnold
Jones, Perry

Kleinschroth, H.
Kovacs, F.
Kozeluh, J.
Kramer, J.
Kukuljevic, G.

Lacoste, R.
Larsen, A.
Lee, H G N
Long, C.
Lott, G.

Macenauer, J.
Mako, G.
Man, A.
Meier, E.
McGrath, V.
McGregor, K.
McNeill, D.
Menzel, R.
Merlin, A.
Metaxa, G.
Mitic, D.
Moldenhauer, H.
Morpurgo, U.
Mottram, A.
Moon, E.
Mulloy, G.

Najuch, R.
Nielsen, K.
Nishimura, A.

Ohta, J.

Pails, D.
Paish, G.
Palafox, G.
Pallada, J.
Parker, F.
Pate, W.
Patterson, G.
Patty, B.
Pellizza, P.
Perry, F.
Petra, Y.
Prentice, B.
Puncec, F.

Quist, A.

Raymond, L.
Reyes, E.
Riggs, R.
Rogers, G.

Satoh, J.
Savitt, R.
Schmidt, U.
Sedgman, F.
Segura, P.
Shields, F.
Sidwell, W.
Stoefen, L.
Sturgess, E.
Sutter, C.

Talbert, W.
Tapi, R.
Tilden, W.T.
Timmer, H.
Trabert, T.
Tuckey, C.

Van Horn, W.
Van Lennep, C.
Van Ryn, J.
Vines, E.
Von Cramm, G.

Washer, P.
Wear, J.
Wilde, F.
Willard, J.
Wood, S.

Yamagishi, H.

V

YEARS	CHAPTERS	PAGES
1951-1968	18-24	101-137